**Women
in America**

WOMEN in AMERICA

Edith Hoshino Altbach

D. C. HEATH AND COMPANY
Lexington, Massachusetts Toronto London

INTRODUCTION

In the past most books on American women were written by men. The male perspective of the author almost unavoidably became a prism distorting his view of the object before him. This situation has righted itself to a degree: *women* are now writing books about women. In the few years since the women's issue became a national concern more books have probably been written by women about women than in the previous fifty years. However, one last distorting lens remains to impair our view. Many of the writers are dedicated feminists; yet, their anger is not the cause of the distorted vision, although it may influence their judgment at times. Most of the authors live in a big city; their metropolitan bias comes closer to the source of the distortion, but the scope of the distortion is wider still.

The plain fact is that most women writing about women have forgotten or never knew what being a woman means for most women. Because of their own select background many women writers have a set of experiences alien to the lives of more unexceptional women. Having been shielded from ordinary female lives by their families, friends, associates, and jobs, these writers may misinterpret or be entirely ignorant of the expectations and values of most women. Enough of a common bond exists among all women to enable women of widely variant life experiences to at least empathize with one another. Yet, the fact remains that much of the literature still depicts a distorted image of what it commonly means to be a woman in America.

The subjects for study in this book are, then, the housewife, both middle-class and working-class and the common working woman. Parts

One and Two on home and the labor force begin with brief profiles showing the substance behind some of the familiar statistics on marriage, birthrates, employment rates, and occupational status. This concentration on housewives and working women turns the attention away from individual women in confrontation with the world or with cases of discrimination and toward the group or class experience of women coping on an everyday level, with their lives. The historical portions of the chapters on home and the labor force are meant to reinforce this collective nature of women's situation: the image becomes one of generations of women working through a vast mire of economic, technological, and social forces, carrying always upon their backs the institutions of home and family.

A faithfulness to "unexceptional" women does not preclude a study of dissent and rebellion. The chapters on feminist movements, past and present, are intended to look beyond individual feminist leaders and organizations to the underlying grass roots sources. The great surge of change during the nineteenth century undeniably produced many exceptional women who made their mark on the successive waves of revolt in the first feminist movement. However, the accomplishments of feminist leaders must be seen as high-water marks amidst the continuous flow of changes in women's situation, in the labor force, and in American culture—changes that anonymous women were living out every day. The greatest leaders in the woman movement of the nineteenth and early twentieth centuries were those women who kept in tune with the lives of unexceptional women. However, the movement itself went another way: as the momentum toward the suffrage amendment grew, the goals of the movement were defined in ever more narrow terms. As a social movement, the drive for suffrage itself probably made its deepest imprint upon the participants.

The chapters on the current women's liberation movement were likewise written with the conviction that the movement grew out of underlying grass roots changes in the lives of uncelebrated women, and that the movement, in order to be successful, will always need to refer back to that underlying base.

Chapter 8 on the issue of day care is a glimpse at how the changing economic and social position of women elicits a response from government, industry, science, as well as housewives and their families. One of the portents of the new day care movement is that it can bridge the gap between typical and "exceptional" women. An issue such as the abolishment of protective labor legislation, long sought by feminists, was not one which furthered a solidarity among women: the struggle for an equal rights amendment to the Constitution which would ban protective labor legislation has been a struggle for and by "exceptional" women. It has not been a cause of the majority of women, although in the end such an amendment may benefit all women. Day care, on the other hand, is a much more tangible and immediate issue for all women. As they struggle to wrest from government and industry the means for day care programs, women are engaged in a collective effort to gain control over their lives for the greater happiness of themselves and their families.

The date chart, which appears in the appendix, illustrates the rhythm and flow of women's history. The juxtaposition of dates concerning household inventions, feminist victories, women's labor statistics, fads and fashions, and miscellaneous events creates a vivid impression of developments in American history affecting women's lives.

Although it is intended as a general introduction to the history of American women, this book is in a way a very personal book. Therefore, it is honest and proper to state a few of the main biases that have guided the selection and emphasis of the book. Three subject areas, for example, receive noticeably brief treatment: single women, women and education, and professional women. The underplaying of these topics is a case not just of simple oversight but rather of calculation.

The status of women in education and in the professions is a worthy subject, and such a study represents one way to approach the condition of women in our society. Because so many of the recent works on women have dwelt upon these topics the author has been influenced to choose another approach. The deciding factor in this matter has been the intent of this book to look for the basic forces of supply and demand, the expectations, values, and need out of which the situation of women has evolved and will continue to evolve. It is in this frame of reference that the educational system and the professional status of women seemed not so much causes as manifestations and symptoms of the position of women in the United States. The status of women in the professions is founded on broadly based economic trends, just as the experience of professional women and the treatment they encounter are part of the essential patterns to women's lives.

The fact that the life situation of women who happen to be "single" is only obliquely touched upon in this text is similarly a purposeful departure from current trends. Only a few of the recent books on women have given more than a nodding recognition to the centrality of the institution of the family to the position of women in society. Most of the recent feminist literature on women and the family attacks the institution as the major stumbling block to the liberation of women. The family *has* limited and guided women, just as men have been limited and guided by their roles in the family and the work world. However, the family has not been a static institution where women are concerned. What the literature does *not* do is to show how the institution of the family has changed as women's place in the whole scheme of society has changed. Although single women are no longer considered the outcast spinsters of earlier periods, the fact remains that the single life is, for women a bit more than for men, still considered a mildly deviant form. No doubt in the coming generation single life will take on new forms, as will family life; the increase in percentage of single women in the marriage-prone years is already an indication of things to come. For the present, however, as in the past, the nexus of roles and experiences revolving around the home remains something with which women must either identify or contend as they try out new roles. Thus, both single as well as married women are pressured and influenced by the ruling economic and social patterns in women's relation to the home and family.

In summary, this book proposes to be a small offering to begin a restitution to ordinary American women. The author has no other justification than the sense of her own ordinariness and the desire to learn how she and other women became what they are. The lives of women in the American mainstream, "unexceptional" women in the sense that they have not been rendered unique and isolated from other women by accidents of background or present circumstance, contain enough rich material for discovery and interpretation to last many lifetimes over.

CONTENTS

Part 3
The Woman Movement

Part 4
The New Feminism

Women
in America

part 1

DOMESTIC LIFE

chapter 1

On the
Home Front
home economics today

Ties of tradition and choice bind women to the home. These ties in themselves justify beginning a book on women with home life. The central position of the institutions of marriage and family for today's women is often obscured. Even though an average of one million additional women enter the labor force each year, women's lives in the home can still reveal much about their situation in today's society. The intertwining forces of supply and demand reach into the home to change both the nature of women's social lives and their work. Throughout history women's lives have changed along with the shifting economic and technological patterns within the home.

The growth of the female labor force should not overshadow the fact that the role of housewife is still the primary occupation for most women. Almost two-thirds of all women in America are *not* listed in the labor force. Most of these women give "home responsibilities" as their reason for not being in the labor force. Furthermore, of the women in the labor force, only two-fifths are full-time, year-round workers. Even women employed at an outside job full time are usually expected to shoulder major responsibilities for home and family. And finally, unmarried women who do not live in a family unit are nevertheless affected by the expectations and restrictions of women's traditional roles as wives and mothers.

The vast body of literature on home, family, and marriage dwells almost exclusively upon the social and emotional functions of the women in these institutions. Woman's place in the home seems to be viewed in an almost timeless way with little regard for historical changes. Most

3

blatantly, the literature on women in marriage and family tends to over-look the background of economic and technological changes against which the social and emotional side of women's functions exist. In reality, women and the institutions with which they are so closely associated can never be separated from the broader structural forces that determine the nature of other institutions.

To give due priority to the economic and technological forces in studying women and the home means, in effect, to extend the concept of "home economics." Home economics, or the "science of home management," must give way to a perspective that treats seriously the ways in which the management of society and the management of the home are inextricably intertwined. Emphasizing this political economy of the home also means going beyond the scope of the U.S. Bureau of the Census and the Women's Bureau in the Department of Labor. For these agencies the home and women's activities within it are not commonly considered part of the work world. Using the vocabulary of the work world may help render more immediate the association of the home and housewives with the external world.

Home Economics

GENERAL JOB DESCRIPTION

Household work is variously described as everything from "busy work" to "unpaid, exploited, and alienated labor." An assessment of house-work is difficult to make because of the proliferation of tasks involved. The work has been labeled "blue collar" by some; yet, and very significantly, it has characteristics that place it apart from industrial work processes and ethics and closer to the white-collar world. At the same time, "home economics" does not fit neatly into either the white- or blue-collar category: first, the houseworker labors solely for the members of the immediate family circle; and second, the work is not subject to the standards imposed by competition that make industrial and commercial work impersonal, utilitarian, and efficient.[1]

The confusion over evaluating housework results from its position straddling several sectors of the hierarchy of work. Undeniably, the housewife's job has similarities with nearly every low-status and low-

[1] Edmund Dahlström and Rita Liljeström, "The Family and Married Women at Work," in *The Changing Roles of Men and Women*, ed. Edmund Dahlström (Boston: Beacon Press, 1971), pp. 19, 32.

paid occupation in society: janitor, maid, baby-sitter, waitress, chauffeur, secretary, short-order cook, and many others. However, there are other aspects to the role that, except in homes of poverty, seem to compensate for the negative features in the eyes of any observer and in those of the housewife herself. The flexible schedule, the chance for frequent coffee breaks, the informal working conditions, and even the privacy are experienced as real benefits if household work is compared to some of the types of work for which housewives might qualify on the job market. And although the woman may object to the social isolation of the job, husbands and school-bound children appreciate the apparent freedom of the housewife to run her own workday.

The peculiar work situation of the housewife has some immediate consequences that are not as enviable. From the point of view of labor, the housewife works in an occupation lacking standards. The work load ranges from part-time to full-time to overtime, depending on the income level, the number of so-called laborsaving devices, the size of the home, the number of children, the style and standard of living. To a great extent the housewife's own working conditions, hours, and pay are dependent not upon her work but upon her husband's income and class. As a laboring class, housewives have real collective grievances.

Among housewives, the prospects for job security, mobility, and seniority vary along class lines. The chances of the premature death of the husband or his desertion or nonsupport of the family are much higher among low-income families than among the rich or moderately rich. Moreover, silent witness to the fact that the law does not provide adequately for the women and children in fatherless homes is the statistical profile on poverty and families headed by women. According to Women's Bureau statistics, families headed by a woman were only 11 percent of all families in 1970; however, they made up fully 37 percent of all poor families. Fifty-seven percent of all poor black families were headed by a woman, and, not coincidentally, almost 25 percent of all female family heads were black. Alimony provisions and laws requiring a husband to support his minor children and his wife (if she is unable to support herself) do nothing for families where there is no money to be extracted from the husband. Furthermore, the situation that exists in some places, in which the mother is forced to file criminal nonsupport charges against her children's father even before she can apply for Aid to Families with Dependent Children, can be very damaging to all sides; the defenseless father, in jail because he has no means of supporting his

5

family, will only be further estranged from the family, and the material improvement to family life is minimal.

Divorce—in and of itself an expensive process—can precipitate the most acrimonious inventory of married life. Whether viewed as reparations, pension, or severance pay, alimony is an issue filled with contradictions, inconsistencies, and inadequacies. Among young couples there is a trend away from alimony. However, for many women in the process of divorce, alimony from the husband continues to be a real need. In cases of financial need—unemployed wife with custody of several children—the housewife depends for her pension or severance pay upon the good will of the husband, the whim of the court, and the aggressiveness of her attorney. In a way, alimony reveals the extent to which the housewife depends on her husband for remuneration for the work she performs.

A divorced woman with children probably has a standing in the marriage-job market that a middle-aged man has who finds himself jobless after being laid off, fired, or having quit his job in a vain search for advancement. Experience on the job goes unrewarded. The divorced woman and the middle-aged unemployed male are damaged goods on their respective markets. Likewise, at the end of their work lives, the man facing retirement and the woman facing an empty house and finding herself with empty hands when the child-rearing and the peak home-making years are over may experience a similar depression. These comparisons signify the comparable commitments that women make to marriage and men make to work.

Continuing the labor interpretation of housework, we may find it useful to look for parallel developments in industry. Before the advent of labor legislation in the U.S., during the first quarter of the twentieth century, most of the occupations of industry and commerce were characterized by flagrantly irregular, unsupervised, and exploitative labor-management relationships. The magnitude of the problems during this period of labor history is, admittedly, a world apart from the scale of work problems confronting most housewives; the two sectors do, however, share difficulties in employee job security, promotion and seniority rights, and opportunities for mobility. After the period of rapid industrial expansion came the period of consolidation, when stability and standardization became crucial. The discovery in industry and business that a contented work force led, in the long run, not only to a more stable and passive but also to a more productive work force, rendered management receptive to reforms and legislation concerning worker welfare. We can anticipate similar trends in home economics.

It can safely be said that the period of expansion in the home economics market has come to an end. This is a relatively new development: as recently as the 1940s and early 1950s, women were praised for their prolific childbearing and proficient homemaking. A period of retrenchment and of public unrest over the economic and social position of the home was inevitable. Increasing signs of rebellion among housewives, their exodus from the home, and the appearance of a feminist revival are parts of this unrest. Reforms in laws and customs regarding marriage and family can be viewed as efforts of the forces seeking to preserve the social order to promote the stability, tranquility, and well-being of the institutions of marriage and family. Identifying housewives as a potentially recalcitrant work force places them alongside previous figures in labor history. Since even housework has a recognized, if veiled, place in the Gross National Product, the comparisons are valid ones.

SPECIFIC JOB DESCRIPTION

Consumption   Consumer goods have virtually replaced the homemade products that the individual family produced under the supervision of women in the preindustrial era. On some tenant farms in parts of the South as recently as the first quarter of this century, women still grew flax for making the family linen. Today, however, the woman must depend almost entirely on what she and her family can purchase. Household production has been removed from the home, leaving in its place mostly routine acquisition, assembly, and maintenance of commodities.

The buying power of a family determines its standard of living. If a family of four has an income of $10,000 or more, consumption will assume for the housewife, at least on occasion, the attributes of a leisure activity and a break from what is sometimes the social isolation of the home. However, if the family belongs to the approximately 10 percent of families living below the poverty level, consumption will be totally devoid of any qualities it may possess for the middle classes, as a diverting pastime in itself.

It is crucial that consumption is one more job over which housewives have very little real control. The housewife functions as purchasing agent for the family. However, as a lone agent, she has scant influence on the market. Beyond developing a cautious attitude of common sense, the consumer regardless of skill or efficiency cannot change the disadvantage with which he or she must operate. Customer demand no longer controls which products appear on the market. The saying that women hold the purse strings of the economy is meaningless, when advertising promotes a standard of living unattainable by many.

The extent to which the advertising industry exploits the image of the housewife should not obscure the phenomenon of consumption that has become a part of the economic, social, and cultural experience in this society. Young adults and children are also high consumers. Shopping has become, for those who can afford it, a mass form of entertainment and leisure; ads and commercials have become a part of contemporary popular culture. The multibillion-dollar advertising industry affects the entire population—not just housewives.

Housework and Appliances It would be shortsighted indeed to attribute the longevity of women's identification with housework solely to the need of manufacturing giants for a happy consumer in each household. This and other popular concepts about the effect of consumer goods upon the work of women at home bear closer scrutiny.

Two of the most widespread beliefs concerning housework are (1) that more household appliances always reduce the amount of work and (2) that this explains the steady growth in the participation of women in the labor force. As for the first proposition, by the end of the first quarter of this century it had already become evident to some observers that the advent of major laborsaving devices and store-bought goods was not liberating women from housework. New responsibilities and expectations were attached to each step away from the old-fashioned way. Laborsaving devices often meant higher standards of cleanliness and diet, and such standards used up some of the time if not the energy formerly expended in backbreaking drudgery. Smaller houses and compact family units have decreased the volume of work in the home but have also left it all to one woman, and perhaps her daughters, to manage.

The second idea—that the existence of laborsaving appliances explains women's entry into the labor force—has been a popular one, now that the steady increase since World War II of married women into the labor force has become a long-term trend. The most obvious counterargument to this would be that in the nineteenth century, when there was a minimum of household appliances even in wealthy homes, working-class married women worked as factory operatives or maids even though they had more drudgery at home than did their husbands.

Conversely, theory number two also fails to explain why as many women do *not* work outside the home today.[2] Lastly, the big jump in the percentage of married women in the labor force came in the period after 1940. If laborsaving devices are to be the main explanation for this rise, it will mean by inference that the first forty years of this century saw little change in housework. Actually, by 1940 the major household devices—plumbing, electricity, modern stoves—were common in urban homes; the changes since 1940 have been mere trimmings by comparison.

Motherhood One thing that remains of women's former productive domestic capacity is the bearing and rearing of children. Yet, the work of motherhood has been altered by the declining birthrate and the increasing responsibility of the school system for the education and care of children.

Recognition of women's economic contribution to society through childbearing has steadily declined as fears of overpopulation have grown. Some social commentators are urging a de-emphasis on the housewife and mother models for women as *the* solution to the population problem. In any case, some de-emphasis appears to have taken place. The latest demographic findings place the fertility rates and birthrates of American women below those of the depression years in the 1930s.

Implicated, but not proven as causes, in these dramatic declines are the availability of oral contraceptives, reforms in abortion laws, the tight economy, a contracted marriage market, as well as the increasing participation of women in the labor force. The marriage market is said to have contracted because women born during the post–World War II baby boom greatly outnumber the men born during the low-birth years of the war and the depression preceding it. Clearly, these trends could all reverse themselves in a short period; however, the facts are that from 1960 to 1970 there has been a decreasing percentage of women marrying. The portion of single women at age twenty rose in that period from 46 percent to 58 percent. At age twenty-one the portion rose from less than 35 percent to almost 47 percent. The changes in fertility

[2] Valerie Kincade Oppenheimer, *The Female Labor Force in the United States. Demographic and Economic Factors Governing its Growth and Changing Composition* (Berkeley: Institute of International Studies, University of California, 1970).

rates and birthrates will have as yet unforeseeable repercussions on the whole economy over at least the next generation.

If one counts the actual physical chores and duties rearing children requires, one discovers that children occupy a decreasing part of the work load of the housewife. A recent study revealed that the average homemaker spends a very small part of her working day in actually supervising and physically caring for her children. Children spend most of their time sleeping, going to school, playing with friends or by themselves. Differences in time spent taking care of children were not great between working and nonworking mothers, although the distribution in child-care responsibilities throughout the workday was more diffuse in the case of mothers who stayed home.[3]

In a manner similar to the survival of housework after the advent of partial mechanization through appliances, the care of children has gained in intensity what it has lost in sheer physical labor. There are fewer children per family now, but the responsibilities of parents for the emotional and intellectual development of each child have added new dimensions to the job.

The change in parental responsibilities was not an abrupt reversal from earlier historical periods; rather the change was one of emphasis. Certainly parents in the preindustrial period were also obliged to oversee the personal development of their children. However, the family contained many members, and bringing up children was mainly the task of passing on the attitudes, skills, and behavior necessary to become functioning members of the family unit. The family was a small production unit, and parental guidance in matters of character and morality was provided in the course of fulfilling the daily work in the family's division of labor.

The modern family, and, in particular, the modern mother, must fulfill the personal nurturing of children who are often separated from the daily activities of the other family members, except during the years of infancy. The major tests and conflicts that children face happen outside the home, in school and on the street, and the mother must mediate between this external life of the family members and life within the family. In this way, parental responsibility for the personal development of children has entered a new phase in the modern period, expanding to fill the void left by the family's vanishing social and economic functions.

[3] Sandra L. Bem and Daryl J. Bem, "Case Study of a Nonconscious Ideology: Training the Woman to Know Her Place." In D. J. Bem, *Beliefs, Attitudes, and Human Affairs* (Belmont, Calif.: Brooks/Cole, 1970).

THERAPEUTICS AND HAPPINESS MANAGEMENT

The new dimensions of the mother's work in the modern period provide a good transition to the last major occupational category in home economics.

Thus far the focus has been on the "blue-collar" aspects of the housewife's job. Other more intangible characteristics of the job have certain similarities to white-collar work. These elements, which might be grouped loosely under the heading of therapeutics and happiness management, have evolved gradually over the decades as the productive functions of the home have retreated, until today in middle-class homes the "white-collar" elements form many a housewife's reason for being. Actually, these are functions of the family as a whole, but, while they are part of the changing experience of men and children today, they affect women more specifically and intensely. The psycho-social job requirements (to retain the occupational terminology of this chapter a while longer) are those that may scar her most deeply and have the most profound implications for all of work and play in our society.

A good example of what is expected of the housewife in therapeutics and happiness management is contained in this passage from a 1961 guide to good housekeeping:

> *The philosophy of* Good Housekeeping *magazine always has centered upon the happiness of the home, not only the spirit but the mechanics. Without the mechanics, the spirit can falter.... The woman who is able to manage the details of housekeeping—which continues to require time and effort even with all the marvelous equipment available—arms her husband against the pressures of twentieth-century business and secures her children with a happy environment.*[4]

This view of good housekeeping has been nurtured by experts on the family as well as by the mass media, such as they have been, throughout the century. Although the language is of a different tone, the words, "The conjugal family . . . has the task of restoring the input-output

[4] *Good Housekeeping's Guide to Successful Homemaking* (New York: Harper and and Brothers, 1961), p. 9.

emotional balance of individualism in job structure,"[5] have the same meaning as the *Good Housekeeping* credo. In this scheme of things, sexuality becomes for the woman an added therapeutic skill—the logical extension of home economics courses and better homes and gardens.

Class Distinctions

Class decides whether the job of housewife is predominantly blue-collar or white-collar. Similarities exist in women's lives through all classes, but class does intervene to demarcate differences in experience and values.

The middle-class housewife lives the white-collar ethic but finds much of her time also spent in doing blue-collar work. Females in truly affluent families have been relieved of all but the most insignificant amounts of blue-collar work. A wealthy woman's primary responsibility to her family is to enhance the family's social standing through her glamour, culture, and philanthropy. These women make a profession of being hostesses, patrons of the arts, and volunteer social workers. They are, in fact, barely recognizable as housewives.

WHITE-COLLAR HOUSEWIVES

White-collar workers and housewives share some characteristic job requirements. Both must sell their personalities as well as their skills or time. In white-collar occupations, this is increasingly true as one goes up the occupational scale. Similarly, middle-class wives and mothers experience a more total wear and tear at their personalities than their poorer counterparts may. As a successful member of the middle class, not only is a wife expected to keep the house clean and provide good meals on schedule, but she may be supposed to accomplish the feat of complementing on the home front the competitive push for advancement that pressures the husband in his job. Not infrequently, the responsibility of the wife for managing the climb toward a higher standard of living, reflecting and augmenting the ambitions of the husband, may be welcomed as a chance to make housework creative and challenging. However, the fact remains that the responsibility puts an added pressure on the woman.

[5] William J. Goode. *World Revolution and Family Patterns.* New York: Free Press of Glencoe, 1963, p. 14, in Cynthia Epstein. *Woman's Place.* Berkeley, Calif.: University of California Press, 1970, p. 112.

It has been observed that the middle-class family extracts conformity both in behavior and in attitude from its members. The good middle-class mother seldom disciplines her children solely to keep them clean, orderly, truthful, or kind. Since so much of their success in life depends upon ambition and self-assertiveness, the mother is anxious that her children acquire such traits. Everyday conflicts become overcharged with significance. The mother may hesitate before ordering her children out of the house should their loud and rough playing bother her, for if she does this, she may be hindering the children's development of an outgoing personality or leadership qualities. Reasoning in this manner, she may, temporarily at least, put up with the noise and mess and disruption of her activities in the home but vent her resentment and frustration later by unnecessarily close supervision of their play or an arbitrary crackdown.[6]

The growth of residential suburbs since World War II is, in part, an extension of the therapeutic view of the home and of women's work. The exodus of middle-class families to the suburbs is, of course, also part of the general historical movement radiating outward from the old urban centers. Suburban life is ideally suited for the therapeutic home. The therapeutic housewife works within the closed family circle to manage the household and to keep personal relationships of family members in delicate balance. Likewise, suburbs offer the hope of realizing the good life by providing the privacy of single-family dwellings and a safe, pastoral, and conflict-free environment.

In the suburbs compulsive work is replaced by compulsive play. The very distance from the places of work—measured every day in the hours spent by husbands in commuting—underscores the withering away of the productive life of the family and of the women within it. Work done by previous generations of women to provide for their families becomes trivialized into hobbies, with men joining in with their do-it-yourself projects. Suburban families are the present-day romanticization of the pioneer frontier of the past—a modern-day matriarchal playground.[7]

[6] Rose L. Coser, ed., *The Family: Its Structure and Functions* (New York: St. Martin's Press, 1964), p. 374.
[7] Lewis Mumford, *The City in History* (New York: Harcourt, Brace and World, 1961), p. 492.

Contrasts between middle-class and working-class homemaking will most clearly show the imprint of class upon women's experience and values in the home.

For the working-class wife or the woman family head living in poverty, the major reality that sets apart her life from that of the middle-class woman is the absence of as many material or financial alternatives. The relentless pressure cannot be alleviated by vacations, baby-sitters, endless streams of appliances and goods. This means that the work of keeping up house and family will require from the working-class woman more personal drudgery and time and energy. Since the work the men in her family are accustomed to getting does not involve the ambition, competition, and manipulative personality, in many cases, that the average middle-class man's white-collar job entails, the working-class housewife's work does not suffer as much by comparison. She will not exhibit quite the apologetic attitude that characterizes middle-class housewives. Moreover, the working-class housewife is providing essential services; she is not merely providing the personal touch to services the family might otherwise be able to purchase in some way—in the form of either more appliances or hired help. Although he may hold more traditional beliefs on the rights of women, the working-class husband is in many cases more willing to share the housework and child care than is the middle-class husband, who can buy his way out of helping by purchasing yet another appliance.

In the working class there is also a much more realistic assessment of the limits to the power of the individual and of the family than is present in the middle class, with its *Good Housekeeping* creed. Absent is the illusion that it is "Molly and me and baby makes three" against the world.

Working-class men are allowed to spend their leisure time with their own buddies to a greater extent than are working-class women. Women, on the other hand, can expect greater support and companionship from their relatives. Although this may lead to a conflict of loyalty between spouses, it does relieve the pressure upon the conjugal relationship to provide all the human needs of man and woman.

What happens to therapeutics and happiness management away from scenes of peace and plenty? Two quotes from the studies mentioned above may underscore the class differences:

> *More than one wife seems to think of her husband less as an individual than as a focus of problems and fears—anxiety about loss of job, disappointment over failure in promotion, fear of conception—the center of a whole complex of things to be avoided. To many husbands their wives have become associated with weariness, too many children, and other people's washings.*[8]

> *An interpretation of class differences in parental values is offered by Melvin Kohn. He characterizes the contrast by saying that "working-class parents want the child to conform to externally imposed standards." The middle classes are more concerned with self-direction and internal dynamics of the child. These differences derive, he holds, from the "entire complex of differences in life conditions. . . of the two social classes," but more specifically from the kind of qualities each requires to get along in the world of work.*

> *Middle-class occupations require manipulation of interpersonal relations rather than of things. They are more demanding of self-direction and less subject to direct supervision than blue-collar jobs. Getting ahead in middle-class occupations is more dependent upon one's own action than upon the collective action of a union.*[9]

It may not be surprising that obedience, neatness, and cleanliness are valued higher the lower one goes on the socioeconomic scale, since these are qualities that relate to standards which can be externally imposed, while higher on the scale, a premium is put on traits relating more to individualism. However, more devastating to an evaluation of the quality of human relationships in middle-class families are the class differences in those values held related to attaining happiness. In the middle classes curiosity and ambition or, in other words, aspiring to knowledge and success are related in the parents' minds to happiness. In the working class, on the other hand, honesty, consideration for other persons, and popularity are the values tied to happiness:

> *Not aspirations for knowledge or for success, but being an honest—a worthy—person; not the desire to outdistance*

[8] Robert S. Lynd and Helen Merrill Lynd, *Middletown* (New York: Harcourt, Brace, 1929), p. 129–30.
[9] Mirra Komarovsky, *Blue-Collar Marriage* (New York: Vintage Books, 1967), p. 77.

others, but, for boys, concern for others' well-being and,
for girls, enjoyment of the respect and confidence of peers:
these are the conceptions of the desirable that accompany
working-class mothers' wishes that their children be happy. [10]

All this is not, however, to erase the similarities between the working-class housewife and housewives of other classes, for, essentially, the isolation and demands of the job are the same.

WELFARE HOUSEWIVES

Women in families that slip below the poverty level experience the most severe reprisals in their work and are treated as if personally responsible for the failure of the family to be an integral and self-supporting unit. The veneer of reverence paid to the family as a private sphere is always stripped away whenever a family falters in its self-support, self-regulation, and self-control—as in the case of juvenile delinquincy or poverty—even though the causes may be beyond the family's control and endurance.

The welfare mother is not treated as an unemployed person entitled to public assistance while seeking a new "position." The welfare mother is rather treated like a worker placed on probation by the foreman because of infractions of regulations and failure to keep up with production. Such a worker may have done nothing more than honestly admit an inability to meet excessive job demands because of faulty machinery or overtime requirements. Or the worker may be one who goes on strike, refusing to absorb the demands of the job. Struggling for survival, the worker may be considered a saboteur. Such is the repute of the woman on welfare.

These women family heads encounter an official policy that contradicts the very basic values of family privacy and integrity that are at the core of our public ideology concerning the family. The privacy and the integrity of the middle-class family are daily subjected to divisive social pressures and the infiltrations of the mass media. However, the welfare housewife experiences these pressures in a direct assault. Social agencies can dictate her life-style, friends, family budget, and personal pleasures. Her life is scrutinized and regulated with a relentlessness that exceeds the power of the most oppressive foreman or jealous husband.

[10]Melvin Kohn, as quoted in Coser, *Family: Structure and Functions*, pp. 481–482.

Certainly the loss of personal freedom the welfare mother must accept is out of all proportion to the financial subsidy she receives, especially in comparison with the amounts disbursed to the giant recipients of government welfare in the business community.

Conclusion

This description of the occupation of home economics has dwelt upon its position in the marketplace of work. As productive labor, housework often goes unrecognized, even though the occupation demands a wide diversity of skills, duties, and mannerisms from the woman. Whether followed as a full-time or a part-time occupation, homemaking demands a resourcefulness not always rewarded in payment of benefits, as in the case of working-class or poor housewives.

Although home economics always entails both blue-collar and white-collar work, the proportion of each varies with the social class of the family. Mechanical aids, working conditions, hours, vacations, and fringe benefits are all decided by family income. Furthermore, the housewife oversees the process by which family members are fitted with the skills and attitudes necessary for success, and these attributes are substantially different in working-class and middle-class families.

The self-image of the housewife is affected by her economic and social situation. Class here works in several ways to influence whether the woman has a high or a low evaluation of her occupation. In a working-class community, a housewife's lot may compare favorably with a man's work life or with outside jobs available to a housewife. The very combination of blue-collar and white-collar responsibilities which enhance homemaking in comparison with many working-class occupations tends to denigrate the status of the middle-class housewife.

Class changes the experience and values: in her everyday life the working-class woman may in practice belie every dictate as to the inferiority of women; yet, she may acquiesce to social or religious beliefs based on the supposed inferiority of her sex. The middle-class wife, on the other hand, may rebel in frustration over even slight wounds to her psyche. Not having been put through the tests of adversity, however, that her working-class or poor sisters have experienced, the middle-class housewife may be more dependent than she would like to admit.

chapter 2

History
of Women
on the Home Front

Today, when the ambiguity of women's work and life in the home is perhaps greater than it has been at any other time, it is difficult to see the real initiative and independence that once characterized women's lives. Yet the history of women on the home front does reveal these qualities. Women's changing lives in the home have initiated and reflected the economic, and social phases through which the nation as a whole has passed.

The Colonial Home Front: New England

Our nation's colonial beginnings provide a logical starting point for examining women in American civilization and culture. While the colonization of this land meant aggression upon the Indian societies already here and enslavement for the soon to arrive Africans, women in the colonial period sharing in a struggle amid primitive material and social conditions, achieved a certain respected status.

LAWS OF SUPPLY AND DEMAND: LIBERALIZING EFFECTS

Obviously, the settlers who founded New England did not come without a history of their own. Moreover, the customs and laws that the settlers brought over from the mother country were explicitly patriarchal. However, the laws of supply and demand in all the colonies and the religiopolitical doctrines in the Puritan areas had a liberalizing effect on the status of women in all spheres of life.

The need for women on the home front in Colonial America was a desperate one. Women were needed to produce and manage the families necessary to populate and civilize the wilderness. Most of the migrants to New England were in family groups; however, in Virginia, where single men predominated initially, great efforts were made by the authorities to induce young marriageable women to settle in the colony. Women were offered monetary reward, property ownership, as well as the lure of almost certain matrimony. In fact, women stood a greater chance of owning property on an equal basis with men during the colonial period than later on. Wives of settlers received land grants in some instances (although the husband would hold the title); widows who were heads of families also received land. The custom in Massachusetts of giving "maid-lots" to single women was soon discontinued lest it induce women to refuse matrimony. There was a thriving and active "wife market," mainly among the poorer classes. This wife market consisted of the many white female bond servants shipped from England. Some were convicts, some were freely indentured servants, and some had been kidnapped and shipped forcibly to the colonies.

Women were valued as contributors of the skills and labor needed to produce food, clothing, and shelter and as managers of family resources and affairs, often in cooperation with the husbands but frequently alone, as in the case of the death, desertion or incapacitation of the man. The functions of the housewife were endless. Women were also highly visible in the social capacities of innkeeper, shopkeeper, school-teacher, and medical practitioner (in this capacity women did everything from delivering babies and diagnosing ailments to discovering and refining medicines). The critical labor shortage made undue attention to defining women's proper sphere unworkable.

The family was definitely considered the basic molecule of society. Logrollings, house-raisings, harvesting, cornhuskings, country fairs, quilting parties, candle dippings, and spinning matches—though sometimes involving primarily the work of the women or of the men—were all occasions that brought out men, women, and children to enjoy cooperative work and sociability. Otherwise the only diversions were church meetings, funerals, and executions. Women did, however, join together in some common labor as when homemakers helped each other over the drudgery and misery of housecleaning by joining forces in a "whang," or cooperative cleaning project.[1]

[1] Eugenie Andrews Leonard, *The Dear-Bought Heritage* (Philadelphia: University of Pennsylvania Press, 1965), pp. 100, 235.

Alice M. Earle, who has recorded much of what is known about the day-to-day lives of "colonial New England dames," wrote thus about old-time American home life:

> *I am always touched, when handling the homespun linens of olden times, with a sense that the vitality and strength of those enduring women, through the many tedious and exhausting processes which they had bestowed, were woven into the warp and woof with the flax, and gave to the old webs of linen their permanence and their beautiful texture. How firm they are, and how lustrous! And how exquisitely quaint and fine are their designs; sometimes even Scriptural designs and lessons are woven into them. They are, indeed, a beautiful expression of old-time home and farm life. With their close-woven honest threads runs this finer beauty, which may be impalpable and imperceptible to a stranger, but which to me is real and ever-present, and puts me truly in touch with the life of my forebears. But, alas, it is through intuition we must learn of this old-time home life, for it has vanished from our sight, and much that is beautiful and good has vanished with it.*[2]

LIFE PATTERNS

In the early settlements the ratio of men to women was 200 to 600 men to every 100 women. Women married young, according to some sources, some as young as 13 or 14, and most before the age of 16. However, by 1790, when there were slightly more women than men, one study of Quaker women places the median age of women at first marriage at 20.5 years. The median age at first marriage of women had risen steadily through the eighteenth century.

After marriage, colonial women could expect an average of seventeen to twenty years of childbearing. For a married couple, then, childbearing and child rearing were the major responsibilities during their marriage. Moreover, since until the late 1800s average life expectancy was under 50 years of age, a married couple could not expect to survive long past the years of child rearing.[3] The perils of childbirth

---

[2] Alice M. Earle, *Colonial Dames and Good Wives* (1890, reprint ed., New York: Frederick Ungar, 1962), pp. 314–315.
[3] Robert V. Wells, "Demographic Change and the Life Cycle of American Families," *Journal of Interdisciplinary History* Vol. II, No. 2 (Autumn 1971) p. 277.

and the diseases of infancy caused a high mortality rate among women and children. The old cemeteries of New England bear silent witness to this. However, if a woman did survive infancy and childbirth and eventually attained the status of widow, she reaped certain rewards for her years of confinement, drudgery, and sacrifice. Widows were the queens of the marriage market; many of them, however, chose to remain unmarried and were to be found in business or other independent professions.

PURITANISM

If the laws of supply and demand gave women's various situations an element of strength and will that was not contained in the traditional dogma on woman's proper sphere, the religion of the new land had a like effect. The Puritanism of New England worked in a subtle way to raise the social status and material conditions in women's lives. These religious beliefs, while extremely repressive in the extent to which they controlled private lives, did ameliorate somewhat the position of the wife. Although marriages were contracted according to very practical and unsentimental criteria, once married, husband and wife were duty-bound to live in mutual affection and respect. From letters of the day it appears that women had some say about whom they would marry, and there was no double standard in the exhortations, at least, to man and wife on their moral duties. True, the husband was the head of the family yet the submission of the wife was to be a joyful one, brought about by the wise and benevolent guidance of the husband. Moreover, if Christian conscience alone did not produce this benevolence in the husband, he was further restrained by laws forbidding him to beat his wife or to force her to transgress against God's law, for as a Christian she was equally responsible to God.

In the theocracy of New England, to a greater extent than in the Southern colonies, the well-ordered family became the very model for statecraft.[4] Letters from seventeenth-century New England show that because of the religious and political interference Puritans had experienced in England, the family for them became increasingly a sphere of privacy and Christian virtue in an alien and wicked world. One of the most revolutionary effects of the Puritan experience was its heightening of the sense of parental responsibility. The family unit was

[4] Edmund S. Morgan, *The Puritan Family: Essays on Religious and Domestic Relations in Seventeenth-Century New England* (Boston: Trustees of the Public Library, 1944).

strengthened. Indeed, many Puritans claimed to have made the journey to America in order to save their children from the sin and decadence of the Old World. In this scheme of things, the New England wife gained the authority and respect due a parent. Within their private home, man and woman did work together to manage their affairs and to raise their children.

The literature on the Puritan North does not support the charge that these New Englanders led a joyless existence. Although private lives were kept under watchful scrutiny in many ways, sensual pleasures were considered a proper conjugal right for both men and women. Women had not yet been relegated to their nineteenth-century vestal virgin status. For example, the custom of bundling as a proper right of courtship—even if it probably was not found in all classes and regions—shows a liberality that was subsequently lacking in mainstream nineteenth-century life.

During the seventeenth and eighteenth centuries some women were always found in visible professions and lines of work otherwise reserved for men. There are instances of women functioning as attorneys and as proprietors and managers of establishments offering every kind of preparation, processing, and disbursement of goods. The range of women's activities shows the extent to which the material economic needs of the country forced changes in the culturally accepted roles of women and hence in social and legal implications of these roles.

However, the patriarchy of both the Southern plantation and the New England Calvinist establishment never relinquished the doctrine of women's inferiority. Public opinion and the laws both supported a male hierarchy that ranked women as auxiliaries to men. Gathered under the authority of family fathers were, depending on the region, livestock, slaves, servants, hired hands, wives, female relatives, and children. Leisure was scarce for men, scarcer for women; wives were often reduced to little more than breeders and general household drudges. Many of the journals and letters of women from the period record lives worn out by unceasing childbirth—often only for the grave—and a regimen of chores without respite. Notices placed by men about their deserting wives were often found alongside notices of runaway horses or cattle. The civil codes still held the power of life and death over women who transgressed against notions revered for thousands of years.

In general, the laws were equally directed against men and women in cases involving adultery and other fornication; however, "punishment of women was generally more severe than that meted out to men . . . and tended not only to be more brutal physically but also to be more destructive to personal integrity."[5] The ducking stool, for example, was purely a punishment for women. The Salem witch-hunt culminating in 1692 did, after all, occur almost in the middle of the colonial period and, since the victims were mainly women, shows how pervasive, even in the New World, were views on the evilness and weakness of women. Even if the extent, numerically and geographically, of the killings was more moderate than that of similar rampages in Europe of the same and later periods, the Salem witch trials must stand along with other infamous cases of persecution, of women and other groups, as an integral part of America's early history.

The fate of Bostonian Anne Hutchinson would be a warning to any rebellious wife or mother as to the dangers of arousing the Protestant inquisition. This woman, an intelligent, articulate wife, mother, midwife, and skilled medical practitioner, was banished from the Massachusetts Bay Colony in 1638 because of her religious teachings, which drew a following and threatened the dominion of the established clergy. The reaction to Anne Hutchinson's religious deviation shows the limits beyond which a wife and mother dared not venture. The laws of supply and demand in the church state could ameliorate much about women's economic, social, and legal status, but only insofar as the greater flexibility in women's roles aided the orderly functioning of civil and religious institutions.

WOMAN'S DOMAIN

During the century and a half of the colonial period, woman's accepted domain—the home—remained at the very center of economic, social, and moral life. Colonial women appear in retrospect to have been wonderfully able to manage their manifold tasks and duties in the domestic areas of home and farm, in social service, or in commerce. This period merits a proportionately long recounting here not only because of its richness regarding women's lives, but also because each new frontier settlement re-created in many ways the situation women faced in the colonial period—at least in terms of material conditions and the harsh demands upon physical stamina and skills. The contributions of women's work to survival and success in both colonial and frontier society is caught in this reminiscence of the Western frontier by a nineteenth-century woman:

[5] Leonard, *Dear-Bought Heritage*, p. 307.

23

I suppose that the most unusual piece of work I ever did
while we were living on the farm was to make a casket for
a little dead baby. . . . Such a way of living is hard, hard,
hard. The only thing that can make it endurable for a
woman is love and plenty of it. . . . I took satisfaction in
the improvements we made, but it seemed to me that our
life grew more burdensome each year. . . . And I couldn't
see much opportunity for my children. . . . Then Dan'l
sold the farm—sold it for $10,000. I've often thought that
a considerable part of that $10,000 surely belonged to me.
All our married life I was just saving, saving. We shouldn't
have had anything if I hadn't been saving. It had been little
better than a wilderness when we took it; we left it in a
good state of cultivation. Those fourteen years seemed a
long time to me, a big price to pay.[6]

The Colonial Home Front: Southern Backwoods and Plantations

The Southern colonies of Maryland, Virginia, North Carolina, South
Carolina, and Georgia were not under the Puritan umbrella, and, because of the plantation system based on slave labor, the experience of
women in that economy and culture was markedly different from that
of women in the North. The conditions and the experience of women
have been quite varied within the South itself. The North did have its
poor and its indentured servants of varying classes; it was not an
egalitarian society. However, the patriarchal controls over women's
lives were relieved by the demands of religious, domestic, and business
spheres that expanded the functions of wife and mother. In the South,
there were three kinds of females: black slave women, backwoods
farm women, and plantation mistresses. The impact of the industrial
revolution to open up jobs outside the home reached Southern women
only in the twentieth century. Therefore, the domestic roles of women
have had a longer maturation period in the South. The lack of major
urban centers to act as catalysts and radicalizers of life-styles and culture
plus the quietude of country life further isolated these women from
changes occurring in the North and in the West.

[6] Harriet C. Brown, *Grandmother Brown's Hundred Years 1827–1927* (Boston:
Little, Brown, 1929), quoted in Mary R. Beard, *America Through Women's Eyes*
(New York: Macmillan, 1933), p. 100.

The slave economy in the South caused both the intolerable economic and psychic, to say nothing of the sexual, rape of black women as well as the entrapment of upper-class white women in the dual role of plantation manager and lady. In addition, it produced yearly new economic and social casualties in the form of indigent white farm families who could not compete in the plantation economy. Slaves could escape to the North, but there they were in alien territory. Until the twentieth century there were few jobs to absorb them.

Only 30 percent of the families of the South could afford to hold slaves at any period; of these, the majority had less than six slaves. Therefore, despite the existence of a slave economy, the actual work life of most white women in the South was little different from that of most women in the North. Diaries of Southern plantation women have, moreover, shown to what extent the image of the Southern belle is a male distortion of reality. The wives of plantation owners bore heavy responsbilities in overseeing the household production of food and goods; wives often had more responsibility than did their husbands in the daily supervision of slave labor in conjunction with the overseers. Their husbands might have been more familiar with the slave quarters at night when they made their sexual invasions, but the wives were responsible for ministering to the needs of the slaves in the way of medicine, clothing, and other personal matters. Writing in the mid-nineteenth century, Mary Boykin Chesnut, born of a wealthy plantation owner's family and married to a high officer in the Army, expressed her frustration at her life:

> Under slavery, we live surrounded by prostitutes, yet an abandoned woman is sent out of any decent house.... God forgive us, but ours is a monstrous system, a wrong and an iniquity! Like the patriarchs of old, our men live all in one house with their wives and their concubines.... Yes, how I envy those saintly Yankee women, in their clean, cool New England homes, writing books to make their fortunes and to shame us.[7]

The Chesnut diary is full of the pain and rage at having to live within the narrow confines of the Southern lady's role in a system whose economic and social decay was becoming ever more obvious. The ideal of

[7]Mary Boykin Chesnut, *A Diary from Dixie*, ed. B. A. Williams (Boston: Houghton Mifflin, 1949), pp. 21 and 165.

"the Lady" came into its full bloom in American society in the nineteenth century, but they were present from the beginning more strongly in the South than elsewhere in the colonies because of the peculiar economic and sexual exploitation of black women under slavery. It has been written that the nineteenth-century male, involved as he was in the materialistic exploits of the business world, was able to reassure himself that he had not "turned this new land, this temple of the chosen people, into one vast counting house" by "reflecting that he had left behind [in the figure of his wife and daughters] a hostage, not only to fortune, but to all the values which he held so dear and treated so lightly."[8] In like manner, the white Southern gentleman set the women in his own family up as "hostages" to purity, piety, and innocence.

In the world of the plantation, the home and the women who ran it were more central to all of work and human association than was true in the commerce-based Northern cities or on the less isolated farms of the North. Though chivalry presumed to place Southern womanhood on a pedestal, the Southern lady was nonetheless immersed in everyday life; she was the bustling center of a small society within her plantation. Even as she was proclaimed the vestal virgin, she was, nevertheless, valued as the producer of the legitimate line of heirs to assure the continuance of white supremacy in a sea of miscegenation.

For the majority of women—whether they lived in the Southern mountains or on the piedmont—their roles in the home tied them to the land in a way that tested their physical and intellectual stamina and ability but did not evolve into a more liberating life.

Summary: The Early Agrarian-based Society

During the period of agrarian-based social and economic values, a period lasting longer in the South than in the North, women were at the center of the institution of the family, which was at once the unit of production, the socializer of children, and the agent of social control. There were class differences and vast discrepancies in wealth, but, except in the South, there was not as yet the polarization of social definitions regarding men and women. Man, woman, and child, while locked into a hierarchy of descending rank as measured in legal and political terms, still were allowed a measure of common experience. Even as the industrial revolu-

[8] Barbara Welter, "The Cult of True Womanhood," *American Quarterly* 18 (1966): 151.

tion had not yet fragmented the work of the family members and generations into more rigid pieces, so there was not yet a whole set of beliefs or cults clustered around the man, the woman, and the child.[9]

Not until the nineteenth century was there a sizable literature on the child and the adolescent. As the agent for social control the family did exact from its members adherence to certain moral standards. It lowered the status of the whole family if one member flouted these standards and, for example, became a drunk or indulged in extramarital sexual adventures. However, this control was not compounded and poisoned by a denial of the sexual nature of women, as came to be true in the nineteenth century, nor, were young men and women kept from all spontaneous association through the rigid segregation and courtship rituals of later times. These new social definitions were results of the rising middle class, and the middle-class definitions of womanhood had little relevance for other classes.

Nineteenth-Century Industrial Society

In the working classes during the nineteenth century, women were forced by material needs to follow the former productive functions of the home into the factories, from which vantage point the social controls on middle-class women seemed irrelevant and self-defeating. The new "Cult of True Womanhood" and the ideal of the genteel lady did not take into account working-class women, just as it did not take into account any of the successive waves of immigrant women. The leisure attained by the middle-class woman resulted in a life-style coveted by all and based on idleness. Once a sin in Puritan society, idleness became a mark of culture and refinement.[10] The working-class woman of the nineteenth century still had what most women had during the colonial and early republican periods of American history: the stimulation and test of personal worth provided by daily, essential hard work shared with other people. The middle-class woman, locked into the new Cult of True Womanhood, could not know the hidden strength of her mind or her own body.

[9] Mari Jo Buhle, Ann G. Gordon, and Nancy Schrom, "Women in American Society: An Historical Contribution," *Radical America* 5, no. 4 (July–August 1971): 3–66.
[10] Gerda Lerner, "The Lady and the Mill Girl: Changes in the Status of Women in the Age of Jackson," *Mid-Continent American Studies Journal* (Spring 1970): 5–15.

GENTILITY: A MIDDLE-CLASS VIRTUE

It is difficult to draw a picture of the life of the sheltered middle-class woman of the nineteenth century. The genteel woman was trained for a passive and withdrawn existence. Nevertheless, historians of the family have brought forth much evidence to show that the Victorian family had undergone changes radical enough to place the middle-class woman in a critical period. Henry Adams wrote that upper- and middle-class women of this period were "much better company than the American man" and "probably much better company than [their] grandmothers."[11] If Henry Adams found these women less complacent and more willing to take controversial stances on subjects close to their lives, it was perhaps because they felt greater conflict in their roles than had previous generations of women. As the family increasingly lost its economic functions, the woman's reason for existing came to be centered more on raising the children and on the surplus functions of guarding values of piety, ethics, and aesthetics. And, correspondingly, as wealth and prestige, for the rising middle class, lay in business and no longer in large land holdings that needed a woman to manage them, the note of success was, as has been mentioned, a life-style of leisure—specifically, the woman of leisure.

The cults of domesticity and gentility presided over by middle-class women served a twofold purpose in the Victorian era: (1) These cults preserved for the developing middle class an arena of legitimacy to offset the pressures from the decadent upper crust and the degenerate lower classes, and (2) these feminine cults gave the woman some measure of power in the home, where the husband was no longer dependent upon her contributions to the home economy as he had been in preindustrial days. However, it must not be thought that the proper middle-class lady of the nineteenth century led a placid existence. This was still a period of nonexistent contraception for most, high infant mortality, unscientific medical knowledge resulting in female ignorance of personal health and hygiene and arduous household procedures.

Alongside the rise of the woman of leisure, the nineteenth century also witnessed a surge of activity directed toward bringing the fruits of "modern" technology into the home. Since this period served rather as a preface to the major influences of technology in the twentieth century, the discussion of early household technology will come later in this chapter.

---

[11] Henry Adams, *The Education of Henry Adams, An Autobiography* (Boston: Houghton Mifflin, 1918), p. 353.

Twentieth-Century Society

DOMESTIC PRODUCTION IN THE WORKING CLASS

Women's productive labor in the household economy did survive the nineteenth century. In the first half of this century women in mill towns and in rural America continued to produce daily with their own hands those things necessary to feed and care for their families, and to barter for additional goods or services. In the coal, iron, and steel regions, a majority of households actually produced much of their own food. Women kept chickens, rabbits, pigs, goats, and cows. In one turn-of-the-century study many families purchased no vegetables other than potatoes, depending instead on their large vegetable gardens. Women preserved, canned, and pickled their produce to ensure a year-round supply.[12]

Moreover, women in working-class families did more than feed and care for their immediate families. A Women's Bureau study in the 1920s of wives in coal miners' families showed that about one-fourth of the wives were gainfully employed, most of them taking in boarders and lodgers. It was estimated that the 376,550 wives in the study were cooking and caring for over one-half million mine workers—more than 100,000 of them as boarders and lodgers.[13] The contribution of the wives was recognized by the husbands and resulted in a sharing of household tasks. Husband and wife in some families shared food preparation and the laundry as well, tasks ordinarily in the woman's domain.[14]

THE SMALL FARM

To look at the lives of small farmers—whether independent, tenant, or migrant—is to look at poverty in most cases. Today the likelihood of poverty among families headed by a farmer or farm laborer is almost as high as among those headed by persons not in the labor force. Of all poor families 27.6 percent are headed by a farmer or farm laborer— the figures are 67.1 percent for poor black families and 23.6 percent for poor white families. To these statistics must be added the uncounted migrant workers' families who have drifted back and forth across the Mexican border during this century.

[12] Robert W. Smuts, *Women and Work in America* (New York: Columbia University Press, 1959), pp. 11–13.
[13] U.S. Women's Bureau, Department of Labor, Bulletin no. 45, pp. 4, 17–18.
[14] U.S. Women's Bureau, Department of Labor, Bulletin no. 74, p. 61.

Small farms make up such a diminishing sector of the work places of America that they and the fate of the people on them are almost invisible. Although small farms have been dwindling as a viable economic venture over a span of a century or more, it is only since World War II that they have reached the vanishing point. Yet, there are still some depressed rural areas in the United States where some desultory farming for a livelihood is carried on—in Appalachia and in the Deep South in particular. Furthermore, the family farm remains as a romantic notion to those women trying to live the old roles of wives and mothers. On a more practical level, learning more about the farm women of our recent past will help balance the picture drawn earlier of working-class and middle-class urban or suburban women of the post–World War II period. Circumstances can vary women's lives so greatly that their roles as housewives are as diversified as their roles in the labor force. Perhaps a brief excursion into the not too distant past will show how, until recently, the work of women on family farms was a whole way of life.

The central feature of the lives of poor Southern farm women during the depression was the never-ending work to eke out a subsistence standard of living. The women had it all to do—the housework, the childbearing, the field work, the tending of the livestock, and the garden cultivating. In their time—the 1930s—their class was already marginal in the national economy; however, within their families these women were major contributors to the survival of the group:

> Quite impressive is the utilitarian and basic emphasis derived
> from an "all work" program. Frills and furbelows, imagina-
> tion and introspection, superficial pursuits have little time
> or place in the thinking and acting of these women.[15]

The work reported in the course of one year by one white tenant farm woman in Texas was somewhat unusual in the variety of work but not in the volume:

    3 weeks—12 hours per day—chopping cotton
    4 weeks—12 hours per day—hoeing corn
    19 weeks—12 hours per day—picking cotton
    15 weeks— 8 hours per day—plowing
    10 weeks— 8 hours per day—cultivating
    4 weeks—10 hours per day—making molasses

[15] Margaret Jarman Hagood, Mothers of the South (Chapel Hill: University of North Carolina Press, 1939), pp. 75-76.

5 weeks—10 hours per day—picking up pecans
52 weeks— ½ hour per day—chopping wood[16]

Included in this woman's schedule is work done for other farmers for wages:

2 weeks— 8 hours per day—chopping cotton, at $1.50 per day
1 week—8 hours per day—hoeing corn, at $1.50 per day
2 weeks—10 hours per day—picking cotton, at $2.00 per hundred-
weight

This woman also hired out one day a week to do people's wash, hauling water for this and all other uses from the river a quarter mile away from the house. The five cows and the chickens produced thirty gallons of milk and ten dozen eggs per week for sale. Her only personal income from all this labor was half the proceeds from the sale of turkeys she raised. She did all the family canning and preserving, buying none of these things from the store. This woman was unusual in that she had only one child. Most women encountered in the Allen study had from six to fourteen children by their mid-thirties.

These were *strong* women. There was no job on the farm that they could not or did not do. In practice they contradicted every notion of male superiority in the biblical edict common to the region. With their labor they subsidized in a real sense the cotton and tobacco industries as much as their underpaid urban sisters subsidized those industries dependent upon mills and factories. The life of work seemed to give these women an emotional maturity unmatched by women of other classes. Yet, time and time again researchers in the Allen study encountered older women who said they would not choose this life if they had it to do over. These older women welcomed the relative freedom and opportunities they saw opening up for women in the cities. They themselves preferred to live in the country and considered the town a dangerous place to raise a family, but they thought it fine that women would not *have* to marry. Research conducted by Ruth Alice Allen revealed that black women were the most bitter in their attacks on men and marriage and the most determined to achieve some economic independence from both.

The turning point for domestic production came with the surge of technological advances accompanying World War II. The lives and work

[16] Ruth Alice Allen, *The Labor of Women in the Production of Cotton.* (Chicago: University of Chicago Libraries, 1933), pp. 98-99.

of rural farm women in the twentieth century are a reminder of how recent are the massive developments which swept the family farm from its position as the central model of American life.

ADVANCES IN HOUSEHOLD TECHNOLOGY

Housework has, it is clear, not shared in the drive toward professionalism and industrialism that has characterized most work in American society. However, housework—and with it women—has not been bypassed by technological developments; moreover, the products of household technology have long been symbols of American affluence in the world.

The surge of home inventions and the drive to reorganize the household led in America to a trend toward advanced household technology that has been unequaled in other countries. Once it was established that there was an ever-expanding market in this country for appliances for the home, the occasional voices raised in favor of a collective answer to housework were drowned out. The scattered population also made collective ventures difficult to execute. In England and on the Continent, on the other hand, the expense and bother of household heating and cooking appliances, for instance, resulted in the institution of the bakehouse. Up until the end of the nineteenth century, it was still common among the lower- and middle-class families to send one's dough for baking and one's joint of meat for roasting to the community bakehouse. Arrangements would then be made for the cooked food to be picked up or delivered at the required time. In France and Germany, two of the major bread centers of the world, bread was never baked at home; to this day in some small German towns, bakehouses exist where housewives can send their bread dough for baking.

The technical capacity to mass-produce appliances to simplify housework did not exist until the twentieth century. However, the urge was there in the late eighteenth and early nineteenth centuries, as reflected by the innumerable patents taken out on household gadgets. Siegfried Giedion has demonstrated with his approach of "anonymous history" the significance of mechanical inventions in revealing a society's undercurrents:

> *Whoever wishes to know what was going on in the American psyche at this time will find evidence not only in American folk-art. The activity of the anonymous inventor is more*

revealing. But only a fraction of the popular habit of invention is preserved in the Patent Office . . . . In them no small portion of folk-art lies concealed. [17]

Giedion cautions against identifying inventions with industrialization. During this period of burgeoning inventiveness, America's industrial capacity lagged far behind Europe's. Nevertheless, from 1865 onward there was a revolution in domestic work, spurred on by the discovery of new power sources in coal fields. This revolution involved gas lighting, municipal waterworks, domestic plumbing, canning, commercial production of ice, improvements in furnaces, stoves, washtubs, sewing machines, and many other advances. Carpenters, blacksmiths, and ho sewives all used what leisure they could find to think up means of modifying old ways of doing things in the home through the use of modern tools—all of which had the goal of providing more leisure. The height of the household inventive surge came during the 1860s. However, before true *mechanization* of housework was possible, the *reorganization* of it had already begun.

By the mid-nineteenth century, there was keen interest in reorganizing the household. The home was inexorably changing from the farmhouse/processing plant as education, industry, and business drew men, children, and women out of the home. Pre-Civil War experiments in modern living were indulged in mostly by reformers of the middle class or by the communistic sects which flourished for a short while. Letters and commentaries from comrades in the abolition and suffrage movements have preserved the record of the Grimké sisters in running a scientific household—following the vegetarian diet of Sylvester Graham—and without servants.

The woman who epitomized this trend was Catharine Beecher, whose book *The American Woman's Home,* written with her sister Harriet Beecher Stowe, became a best seller. Catharine Beecher was the perfect example of a Victorian woman steeped in all the traditions of the Cult of True Womanhood, a member of the weaker but purer sex who, because of the exigencies of middle-class existence, was forced to go outside of woman's "proper" sphere to earn her own livelihood. She solved her predicament by making a life's career out of female education—education for the true vocation as wife and mother, but education also,

[17]Siegfried Giedion, *Mechanization Takes Command, A Contribution to Anonymous History.* (New York: W. W. Norton, 1969), pp. 40–41.

should fate decree it, for those occupations such as teaching for which women, it was thought, are innately suited. Servants were in short supply; therefore she combined her household reforms with the creed that the small, efficient, independent household was the core of a democratic society, leading us away from feudal times when one person would have to slave for another. She took due note of the trend toward the professionalization of occupations and stressed that her sex's only salvation was to receive a professional training for woman's vocation. She founded home economics as we know it today. Her approach to problems facing modern families was to seek reform in each individual home through education and technical improvements. The individual, not collective, approach was to be the standard for the next century.

The next stage in the reform of housework was the scientific reorganization of the work process that occurred after 1910. By 1914, profit figures of those industries producing household appliances showed that the middle-class woman was probably having an easier time at home. *After* the mechanical appliances had been accepted on a mass basis, the efficiency experts, the time-and-motion-study people turned their attention from the factory assembly line to the kitchen. The streamlined kitchen (which had already been engineered by them for the railroad's Pullman cars) eventually looked not a little like the continouous-work-space kitchen that Catharine Beecher had so carefully blueprinted.[18]

One lesson of this brief history of housework is that there had been a steady drive to bring housework up to the standards being met by other work, to make it creative, efficient, even professional. Thus, it is not the post–World War II advertising executives who "subverted" female minds and emotions, urging women to find fulfillment and satisfaction in housework. Rather, the whole thrust of recent history has been to reform housework through technology in the individual private home, with women ideally in full-time charge.

By 1920, then, there had been quite a change: in the large cities, sales of canned foods were up, delicatessens had expanded with the urban population, and the bakery business had also multiplied. Reformers such as Alice Henry and Charlotte Perkins Gilman looked forward to the time when household chores would be specialized out of the home through technology. An almost irrational faith arose on many sides in the power of technology to correct all human inequities and

[18]Giedion, *Mechanization Takes Command,* pp. 9, 519.

solve all problems. These reformers believed that just as the uncertainties facing women were the result of some unfortunate "cultural lag," so the problems of housework would also be solved once scientific organization got around to the home. In Alice Henry's words:

> Is it not strange that she with whom industry had its rise and upon whom all society rests should be the last to benefit by the forces of reorganization which are spiritually regenerating the race and elevating it to a level never before reached?[19]

Charlotte Perkins Gilman wrote in an article:

> . . . now when the ballot does not free woman from economic dependence, and when economic independence can not be maintained by the wife and mother until her household labor is professionalized, that immense structural and functional change in our economic base, the home, begins to loom large before us.[20]

Yet, the fact remained that the final step had not been taken—the transformation of housework into a regular occupational category through industrialization, true professionalization, and community services. Perhaps everyone resented the idea of such an intrusion into the intimate sphere of life, or perhaps women's time was just not computed to be worth all the social upheaval such a transformation would entail. In 1911 the American Statistical Association estimated that home cooking was from 30 to 55 percent cheaper than that of restaurants and bakeries—with the housewife's time being estimated as worth 8½¢ per hour. That 8½¢ was *less* than the unskilled women operatives in the Pittsburgh metal industries were earning![21]

From the mid-1930s on, American industry began to concentrate on the streamlined kitchen and continuous work space. Lillian Gilbreth (who was made famous as the mother in *Cheaper by the Dozen*), the production engineer and efficiency expert, studied the American kitchen

[19] Alice Henry, *The Trade Union Woman* (New York: D. Appleton, 1915), pp. 242-243.

[20] Charlotte Perkins Gilman, "Where Are the Pre-War Radicals," *The Survey*, February 1, 1926, p. 564.

[21] Frank H. Streightoff, *The Standard of Living Among the Industrial People of America* (Boston: Hart, Schaffner and Marx Prize Essays, 1911), p. 88.

and concluded that manufacturers did not know what housewives needed and that housewives knew neither what they needed nor what they wanted in kitchen design. Home economics texts of the 1940s and 1950s abound with detailed descriptions and analyses of work processes, traffic patterns, and appliances in the kitchen and other work areas of the home.

To an overwhelming extent, the housewife's dilemma, as it was sometimes called, was seen as a problem to be solved by rearranging appliances and rooms within the home—rearrangement of people and their roles within society was given infinitesimal attention by comparison. For instance, in the middle-class home the isolated kitchen, separated if possible by a pantry from the dining room, was a relic of the days when servants were a commonplace. The housewife in the servantless household felt isolated under this room arrangement. The twentieth-century solution was to connect the kitchen to the dining room by means of a window or even by doing away with an intervening wall. In some houses designed by the Frank Lloyd Wright school of architects, the kitchen is in the center of the house, separated only by curtains that can be opened at will from the other rooms, which flow outward from the kitchen in pie-shaped wedges.

The modern kitchen is the end product of the reform movement begun by Catharine Beecher and her anonymous contemporaries. However, the housewife's dilemma was not solved through the efforts of this long-lived movement. Lillian Gilbreth was a brilliant engineer, and her work in modernizing the American kitchen has probably made housework at least less tedious for millions of women; however, her reasons for encouraging women to become more efficient housewives seem strangely unconvincing. Her statement also suggest the contradictions that continue to exist in woman's role as housewife:

> Many remedies have been suggested. Most of them, however, seem to suggest that the best way for woman to improve her lot is to escape from it.
>
> This is fallacious—first of all because she doesn't really want to escape from it, and secondly because it is obvious that somebody must and should do the work. . . .[22]

---

[22] Lillian M. Gilbreth, Orpha Mae Thomas, Eleanor Clymer, *Management in the Home* (New York: Dodd, Mead, 1959), p. 3.

Conclusion

This chronicle, past and present, of the home front has shown women when they lived to the fullest the traditional roles of wife and mother. In many respects, women in the home today are living in the afterglow of the past. Through almost four centuries of American history the central position of women to home and family has endured, at the same time initiating, reflecting, buffering, and guiding changes in the economic, political, and social structure of a developing country.

Simone de Beauvoir, at the end of a long treatise on the injurious effects upon woman of her sphere in life, made a telling distinction between housework and the male work world that perhaps more than any other observation explains the longevity of women's position on the home front:

> *Cooking, washing, managing her house, bringing up children, woman shows more initiative and independence than men slaving under orders. . . . The woman gets more deeply into reality. The baby fed and in his cradle, clean linen, the roast, constitute more tangible assets; yet just because, in the concrete pursuit of these aims, she feels their contingence—and accordingly her own—it often happens that woman does not identify with them and she has something left of herself. Man's enterprises are at once projects and evasions: he lets himself be smothered by his career and his "front."* [23]

Thus, by a sort of negative reasoning, we find that, because of the very fact that household work is not all-absorbing and fully satisfying, the woman retains something of her selfhood; while generations of men may have lost themselves in their careers, women continue to operate within the home, delving deeper into reality and emerging with a greater sense of self. This common experience of women is one that bridges barriers of class and time.

[23] Simone de Beauvoir, *The Second Sex* (New York: Bantam Books, 1961), p. 588.

part 2

THE LABOR FORCE

chapter 3

WOMEN AT WORK FROM MILL TO OFFICE

Although the economic and social patterns of women's lives on the home front determine what it means to be a woman in American society, the direct imprint upon women of another factor, the nation's labor force—as a source of opportunity and an area of participation—is deepening. Behind the recent statistics documenting the continued increase in the participation of women in the labor force throughout most phases of their lives lie both choice and force of circumstance. For some women employment is now, and has been in the past, one way to gain the initiative in economic and social affairs that may elude them in the home. However, the broader forces accompanying and guiding the extent and nature of women's employment have involved more than personal ambition or personal financial need. In the end, women's labor force participation has been a function of some of the same system-wide economic and technological trends that lay behind the changing roles of women on the home front.

In the years since World War II the margin of choice has been extended, allowing women more flexibility in deciding how they will occupy themselves in the successive phases of their lives. As the chapters on the home front have indicated, the realities of responsibilities and expectations with which women live as wives and mothers determine most of women's potential and opportunity. However, the dichotomy between marriage and family on the one side and a job or career on the other has become less marked.

In the following discussion, we will couple a look at current profiles of women in the work force with a historical review. For, as will be shown, the major trends in women's labor force participation and distribution through the occupational groups had their origin in the last quarter of the nineteenth century. There is merit in chronicling women's long and diverse labor history in and of itself; however, more essential for grasping women's situation in the world of work will be the interpretation of trends both past and present, including such points of reference as the growth of the textile industry and the needle trades, the emergence of class distinctions in employment, the expansion of certain sectors of the labor market, and the changing consciousness among employees.

Problems of Perspective

Taking the broader, historical view forces a modification of some commonly accepted perspectives on women and the labor force. This chapter will seek to avoid both the primarily optimistic and the primarily pessimistic viewpoints.

The first perspective that needs modification is that of the U.S. Women's Bureau in the Department of Labor, which accentuates the numerical gains women have made in the labor force and interprets these as signs of the growing power and well-being of working women and of the country as a whole. It is in fact, however, a distortion of women's position in the nation's economy to equate the increasing labor force participation of women with their liberation. Whereas the opening up of the job market to women creates options that women in earlier periods may have had only in restricted numbers, it could be argued from several points of view that women's overall status in the labor force has declined since the beginning of the century.

The second perspective that must be tempered in order to do justice to the situation of women in the labor force is the one that views them solely as victims of social and economic discrimination as workers. The discrimination and the exploitation exist and are not here at issue. However, an analysis of women in any sphere of their lives that concentrates on their victimization misses several things. As applied to the labor force, the victim theory of women's situation negates the strength of women who have endured as workers, isolates sex discrimination from that on other grounds, and leaves unrevealed the multiple ways in which women's economic roles have been formed historically.

Encumbering the appraisal of women workers from any perspective is the deceptive quality of data on women. A recent article refers to a "statistical-industrial complex" that hides the truth of women's position in the labor force by means of contrived definitions and categories. Included in this complex of interest groups are some government agencies and departments, the business and industrial community, independent educational and research foundations, politicians, and portions of the mass media.[1] At issue are critical statistics on levels of poverty, unpaid work, unemployment, and underemployment.

The statistics on the female labor force not only fail to report the problem areas but also leave hidden certain groups of working women. The main group of hidden working women is to be found in family businesses. It will probably never be known how many women labor beside their fathers, brothers, and husbands to run the thousands of small businesses that come and go annually. Lack of information, misinformation, and deceptive information combine to obscure the true situation of these and other women in the labor force.

Problems of data exist in any study, and it is not unique to our particular area that statistics are incompletely or deceptively reported to serve the political needs of powerful interest groups. It would therefore be unwise to dwell heavily upon short-term shifts in women's position in the labor force. Too often pronouncements on sudden great leaps forward in women's employment are revealed upon closer scrutiny to be only the belated official recognition of trends originating in previous decades.

Profile

WOMEN IN THE WORK FORCE

On the surface, the profile of the female labor force is easily drawn with a few figures. The almost 32 million working women in the United States today constitute 38 percent of the total labor force. Of these working women 60 percent are wives, 38 percent are mothers. While women are present in at least token numbers in most occupations, they are concentrated in the clerical and service occupations. As a sizable minority, women are represented in jobs as factory operatives and in technical and professional work. However, aside from the 4.3 million women in technical and nominally professional fields, female workers are clustered in occupations traditionally low in status, in pay, and in

[1] Betty MacMorran Gray, "Economics of Sex Bias: The Disuse of Women," *Nation,* June 14, 1971, pp. 742–744.

opportunity for advancement. Within occupations themselves, work tends to be divided into jobs for men and jobs for women, often with corresponding discriminatory pay scales.

Women's place in the job hierarchy results in median earnings (for full-time, year-round jobs) that are only three-fifths those of men. The discrepancy between the sexes in earnings has increased since the 1950s. Similarly, almost without exception, the unemployment rate for women has been much higher than that for men every year. Moreover, continuing the pattern, the gap between the sexes in unemployment rates has also widened since the 1950s. To round out this brief profile of the female labor force, we should add that women amount to less than 20 percent of the labor union membership, although they are nearly 40 percent of the work force.

Two causative factors lie behind the percentages in this profile of the female labor force. On the one hand there is the direct and often exploitative discrimination that denies women both equal work and equal pay. The record of blatant abuse of women workers needs only to be exposed to be comprehended. The other factor accounting for women's rather tenuous situation in the labor force can less readily be labeled simple exploitation. This second factor consists of the interplay of several job market trends. The way in which three such trends converge upon one another to shape women's work lives can serve as an illustration here: Three of the trends characteristic of the female labor force in the decade following World War II are the expansion of clerical and service occupations, the rise in part-time work, and the accelerated entry of married women into employment. These three trends are totally interdependent. The supply of labor power among married women met the demand of the expanding job market; and the supply of jobs met the demand of married women for employment.

Thus the participation of women in the work force assumes a more utilitarian and a more contingent character: women are in the work force not so much by virtue of their own initiative as by the grace of an increased demand that they happen to be able to meet.

SUPPLY MEETS DEMAND

The postwar period saw the great expansion of clerical and service occupations at a time when certain sectors of the labor force were con-tracting. Because of the low birthrates of the 1930s, fewer young per-sons were available to replenish the labor supply. Moreover, more young men and women were dropping out of the labor force or delaying entry into it in order to seek higher education. Older workers, those over sixty, were retiring to a greater extent than before.

The new jobs were not highly skilled ones, but they did require a certain level of education and training—high school, preferably some college, and possibly some vocational training. Moreover, these were sometimes part-time or seasonal jobs. It was under this set of circumstances that married women became attractive to employers seeking workers to fill the new jobs. As waitresses, hairdressers, bank clerks, receptionists, computer-card punchers, and secretaries, increasing numbers of married women entered the labor force.

In a pattern to be encountered in other periods, public opinion on the idea of women working—especially married women— has undergone a steady liberalization since 1945 as the need for workers increased. Women have always worked in one way or another, but work *outside* the home became quite acceptable to much of the population. (The debate on whether married women should work—where such a debate exists at all—now revolves around the welfare of the children and has lost most or all of the earlier moral or ethical overtones, except for some ethnic minorities with traditional values.)

Thus, the special nature of the female labor force consists in the jump in the proportion of its members who are married. In 1971 almost 60 percent of all women workers were married—as opposed to 30 percent in 1940. The median age of women workers has risen steadily in the postwar period—from age thirty-two in 1940 and age forty in 1968. The assumption has been that these new employment patterns have been mutually beneficial to employers and married women workers. However, closer examination may persuasively show that while married women provided a highly suitable new supply of labor, the jobs offered them were not equally suitable to these workers. Our two points of focus in this evaluation of women in the work force will be part-time work and the motivations of those seeking employment.

PART-TIME WORK

Whereas most female part-time workers give household responsibilities and their children's school attendance as their reasons for not working at a full-time job, they have not always arrived at this work pattern by choice. Countless women work part time only because they cannot find full-time, year-round employment—either because such work is closed to them on account of lack of training or arbitrary discrimination, or because in their community full-time work is sporadic and seasonal. This predicament is prevalent among women who work as private household workers or as waitresses or cooks. Patterns of part-time work can indicate severe underemployment.

The whole area of part-time employment needs investigation. Management sometimes complains that part-time workers cost more than they are worth because they increase the overhead. More recently, however, women have suspected that business and industry find part-time and temporary full-time workers a profitable way to avoid paying costly fringe benefits and raises in wages. Furthermore, this practice of keeping workers on a temporary basis is believed to occur with the approval of some unions, which receive union dues from these short-term workers; because these workers are dismissed before the probationary period is over, the union does not have to provide the union benefits that longer term members are entitled to. At the very least, it would be premature now to assume that part-time work or temporary or sporadic employment has been tailored to suit the lives of women.

WORK MOTIVATION

Traditionally it has been assumed that women work because they are forced to by economic necessity. The Women's Bureau, which has maintained an admirably protective attitude toward working women throughout its fifty-year existence, has, until very recently, stressed only the economic need of women workers. Whereas men are *expected* to work, the motivations of women workers have always been a topic of public discussion. The conflict between idealized images of women as wives and mothers and the concrete demands of the marketplace reasserts itself periodically in the public discussion on women and the labor force.

The older feminist organizations and professional women's groups have reacted against the emphasis on economic need, claiming that women should and do work for the same variety of reasons as men. Such women say that for women, as for men, economic need is but one motivation among others—such as desire for success, recognition, creativity, contact with people. Given the fact that the isolated home does not always allow the satisfaction of many of these needs, it is likely that many women take jobs for completely nonfinancial reasons.

Yet, economic need is still a large part of why women work. For the sake of the record, if one judges on the basis of marital status and family income, it can be said that by the usual economic measurements, the majority of women in the labor force work out of necessity. Women in the labor force who are single, divorced, widowed, or separated can be assumed to be self-supporting for the most part. Working women whose husbands have meager or barely sufficient incomes also have an economic need for employment. The fact that women with husbands whose incomes fall below the poverty line are more apt *not* to work than are the wives of husbands at higher income levels is a special case to be examined shortly. To complete the tabulation, using 1971 figures, we must conclude that a total of 20.7 million women in the labor force appear to have pressing and immediate financial reasons for working, regardless of other motivations.[2]

In the middle class, women are propping up the staying and buying power of American families. For a long time, women whose husbands' earnings were in the lower- to middle-income level had the highest rate of labor force participation. Now, however, there is evidence that the rising cost of living and the failure of wages to keep pace have sent more women from solidly middle-class families into the work force. This trend holds for nonwhite as well as white middle-class families.

The overburdened working-class woman who works all day at home and then most of the night cleaning offices is still a reality. Some women still take in piecework to do at home, struggling to make the money for the family's next meal or pair of shoes. The figures on working mothers outline a picture of economic necessity. The presence of dependent children generally lessens the likelihood that a woman will work outside the home, especially if the children are under school age. However, if the husband's income approaches the official poverty level or if the husband is not present or is unable to work, the percentage of mothers who work, regardless of the age of their children, rises dramatically.

It is true that the shorter workweek for men and the existence of part-time work for women have enabled many couples to take care of the children and keep house in shifts. However, there are expenses related to the job that eat away at a woman's potential meager income. The Women's Bureau lists such costs as those incurred for clothing, personal care, food, transportation, child care, household help, and taxes and states that these may consume from one-fourth to one-half of the wife's earnings. Moreover, the wife's income may place the

[2] "Why Women Work." U.S. Department of Labor. Women's Bureau. Government Printing Office, 1972.

family's total income in a higher income tax bracket. Thus, some women may not be able to afford a job!

SUMMARY: WOMEN AT WORK

The overriding impression one is left with is that women have a very tenuous position in the labor force today. The ways in which women exist in the job world show both tenacity and resignation in the face of many hardships and obstacles. Women have been in turn indispensable troops and surplus fodder in the labor force. Alternately submitting to and withstanding the peculiar combination of forces stemming from their roles at the workplace and in the home has been women's experience in the modern period. Yet, the situation of women in the labor force is not a static one, as even this brief overview of the immediate postwar period suggests. The restrictions, points of stress and opportunity have their origins in the labor history of American women.

The rise in the number of married women who seek work outside the home is but one instance of trends that have links to the past: explanations for the currently high number of married women workers are tied to reasons for the steady acceleration of women's entry into the labor force since World War II. And the major trends that determine women's labor force participation today go back, as mentioned earlier, to the last quarter of the nineteenth century. Of these trends the most important phases were the move away from farm labor and, subsequently, the shifting distribution of female labor among domestic service, industrial occupations, and white-collar work. With the growth of the educated female working force, domestic service lost ground to industry, which, in turn, gave way to the emergence of the white-collar sector as the one with the greatest potential for utilizing women.

Women's Labor History

It may not be as universally true as it once was that woman's work is never done, yet, women have always in all periods of American history earned their keep, both materially and figuratively, according to the cultural usages of the day. On the home front women held the lifeline of the new country in their bodies and in their hands. Virtually all productive labor was once centered in the home, under the guidance and as a result of efforts of women.

WANTED: CHEAP LABOR

In response to the almost insatiable demand for labor, the early settlements in this country were launched with the support of added sources of cheap labor. In the North the extra labor power was provided by indentured servants, many of them women. Their lives while in service must have resembled a period of probation. Tales of sexual exploitation of female servants are not lacking. Marriage and a regular family life were often not possible for these women; however, should they bear a child, they could expect to find themselves in debt to their masters or to the town for the "damages," or loss of labor, they had caused while indisposed by childbirth.

The other source of cheap exploitable labor was black slaves. In those regions where cotton or tobacco were the main cash crops, slaves formed the foundation of the economy. In the neighboring regions of the South, slaves themselves were the cash crop. Not only did men and women labor without pay but even the products of their own bodies—their children—were often torn away and sold. Black slavery will stand as the most extreme form of labor exploitation and total oppression of a people. Because of the expanse and wealth of this country's resources and markets, the need for a cheap and readily available labor source would remain constant throughout the various periods of expansion. If the labor source was not present, labor was brought to the plantation, railroad construction site or factory; if this failed, the industry followed the labor source.

COTTON MILL GIRLS

The transition from a rural economy with individual home industries carried on by the women of the family to factory manufacturing in the town became highly visible with the opening of the first viable cloth mills in New England in Rowley, Massachusetts, as early as 1643. By the nineteenth century enough capital, often supplied by local governments, had been amassed to set up small operations in New England, thus moving the making of clothing farther from the home and concentrating it in the cloth-making factories.

A debate on the need for manufactures in this country and their possible effect on agriculture had been in progress since the 1790s at least. Numerous authorities had agreed by the first quarter of the century that the development of manufactures was crucial to the prosperity and security of the nation. The War of 1812 had placed the future supply of cloth from England in jeopardy. The production of cotton cloth appeared to be a most advantageous industry for the United States, and, after several short-lived attempts, a profitable factory was established in Waltham, Massachusetts in 1814. To counter the charge that the development of such manufactures would "divert labor from the land," the "Friends of Industry" were quick to point out that women and children were most suited to such work and that since their labor was nonessential and actually inefficient on farms, their entry into the mills would result in a generally more complete utilization of the country's labor power.

At a time when much strenuous and creative work was still centered in the home, women's part in this work was belittled, deprecated in public pronouncements as mere "idleness." One would have found not idleness but rather the vain labor of many hands on the New England farms then failing thanks to generations of families who had extracted the nutrients from the soil but never replenished it. Publications from that period are replete with references to the useful and profitable occupation of mind and body that the mills afforded women who would otherwise lack financial support or "eat the bread of idleness." Women were not the only potential labor force thus courted. Children were also sought after as a cheap and available work force for the mills, as they were everywhere in these years long before child labor legislation. The old Puritan ethic of the virtue of industry, which had been applied to men and women alike in the New England theocracy, was used in this campaign to sway public opinion in favor of the employment of women and children in the factories. In the words of the propaganda, women were merely passing from the "wise and benevolent" supervision of the men in their families to that of their "captains of industry."

THE "ROMANCE" OF THE FACTORIES

However, for the predominantly female textile workers, the mills did mean a step toward independence and self-determination. No longer dependent upon their families for their livelihood, young women could send money home and still accumulate some savings.

It has been said that, in a sense, the mills, and the Lowell, Massachusetts, mill in particular, because of its image as a model institution, were the women's colleges of the day. Middle-class young women came to the mills for every reason: very soon the emphasis was shifted from the moral advantages of work in the factories (the decisive sectors of public opinion having already been convinced) to the adventurous, refined, and romantic aspects of such labor. Despite this self-serving propaganda, the fact remains that the women who flocked to the rapidly expanding textile industry provided by their own example new models for the proper roles of women. And the trend toward work for women away from the home did contain that element of liberation.

In 1816 approximately 66,000 women and girls and 34,000 males (two-thirds of them boys) were employed in the cotton industry. It has been said that "both machinery and morals at the Lowell mills were planned for the employment of farmers' daughters who wanted to earn money."[3] There was no social stigma involved in the work; as yet no class lines had formed for women's work outside the home, there being so few options. During this time—the 1820s and 1830s—the mills of New England were hailed as models for the international industrial community to follow.

Behind the facade of this auspicious start to women's industrial labor were realities that did not set a good precedent for the consciousness of women who were, in time, to form the working class. It did not escape the notice of manufacturers that, with or without picturesque settings, the women were still willing to work from sunrise to after sundown, by candlelight if necessary in winter. Wages were low, and a woman had to work a full twelve months and give two weeks' notice before quitting or else forfeit her "honorable discharge."

New Conditions, New Consciousness By the mid-1830s these quaint qualities of the working women of Lowell and other mill-company towns had become galling to some, both inside and outside the industry. In 1836 a Committee on Female Labor made a report that mocked the charitable activities carried on by socially-minded women, pointing out their failure to attend to the oppression so close at hand:

> *Is it not singular that females who would sacrifice their time and health to distribute tracts and collect moneys for the heathen could not devote a mite for their own oppressed countrywomen? . . . while they are discharging the*

[3] Elizabeth Faulkner Baker, *Technology and Woman's Work* (New York: Columbia University Press, 1964), p. 10.

duties of humanity they should not overlook their own sex and kin.[4]

Very sporadically through the twenties and thirties and with growing militance in the 1840s, women in the mills staged walkouts and began to form more lasting organizations. By mid-century, the mills of New England were vastly changed. In its closing editorial, *The New England Offering,* the Lowell mill paper, edited by mill operatives, recorded the new situation and the new consciousness:

> *We have been accused by those who seem to wish us no ill. . . of unfaithfulness to ourselves as exponents of the general character and state of feeling among the female population of this city. They say the* Offering. . . *does not expose all the evils and miseries and mortifications attendant upon a factory life. It speaks, they say, on only one side of the question; and they compare us to poor caged birds, singing of the flowers which surround our prison bars, and apparently unconscious that those bars exist.*[5]

What had happened at Lowell and elsewhere was that the wages and services offered by the early mills no longer ranked above the standards for industrial work. There were other industries competing for their share of the labor market. Moreover, other opportunities were opening up for women, in teaching and in settling the West. Operations within the mills themselves had been transformed and speeded up from the 1840s onward through technical innovations, which also increased the noise, dirt, and heat.

Simultaneously, the working population in the industry was undergoing a radical change. Whereas in the 1820s females had made up 90 percent of the work force, by the mid-1850s one-half the mill workers were Irish men and women, driven from their country by the potato famine. Therefore, the manufacturers were able to draw upon a fresh labor supply, one untouched by the emerging female labor movement

[4] As quoted in Hannah Josephson, *Golden Threads* (New York: Duell, Sloan and Pearce, 1949), p. 239.

[5] *The New England Offering,* A Magazine of Industry Written by Females Who Are or Who Have Been Factory Operatives, 1845-1850, 3 vols., ed Harriet Farley, 1: 376, as quoted in Edith Abbott, *Women in Industry* (New York: D. Appleton, 1910), pp. 130-131.

that had risen in the 1840s to challenge the exploitative treatment of women in the industry. In wages, hours, and conditions, the industry was worse in the second half of the century than it had been at the start. By 1900 women were but 42 percent of all workers in the cotton textile industry, although more women than ever before—nearly 127,000—were mill workers.[6]

The South In its relentless search for cheap labor, much of the cotton textile industry moved to the South, traditionally the area for the cultivation, not the processing, of cotton. With the tapering off of immigration after the turn of the century and the passage of anti-immigration laws in the 1920s, the South became the last pool of unemployed, unskilled labor. Moreover, new technical developments in loom machinery were being introduced, and it was more economical to build new plants than to remodel the old New England mills.

The South was still a largely rural region after the turn of the century. The ties to the land were strong, and farming was a way of life imbedded in the culture of the people. There was opposition to the arrival of big industries, and, not really surprisingly, some of the same arguments resurfaced that had been used to woo Yankee farmers' daughters into the mills in the early 1800s. People wishing for the industrial development of the South purported to see idle women and children everywhere in need of the schooling of industrial labor.

The new technology transformed the ratio of skilled to unskilled labor, raising the proportion of unskilled work. There was a corresponding rise in the percentage of women and children in the industry, since they tended to be drawn into the unskilled areas.

The mill towns that were established in the South in the early decades of this century attracted poor whites from the piedmont and the coastal plains who had been impoverished by exclusion from the plantation system, and mountain whites driven by unproductive farms from their generations of isolation. Whole families descended upon the shabby mill towns to try to make a living. Millwork tended to absorb all available family labor power. Children of age were either working in the mills (and often missing schooling) or taking care of the younger ones so that mother and father could go to the mills. In one study from the 1920s, about one-half the families had one wage earner, over one-fourth had two wage earners, and almost another one-fourth had

[6] Baker, *Technology and Woman's Work*, pp. 17, 114.

three or more. Of the 971 workers in this study, 32 percent were female. In all, 60 percent of the families had female wage earners.[7]

The South was still producing much of its cotton in the pre–World War II days on farmers' small holdings and on tenant farms. Farm labor is one of women's traditional occupations; in 1900 it ranked second, after domestic service and ahead of industrial labor, as the employer of women. It was estimated that in Texas alone, the unpaid labor of women on tenant cotton farms produced one-thirtieth of the total crop.

The alternate cash crop of the region was tobacco. Many small farmers lived close to the poverty level, going into debt year after year to raise a crop that they could not even eat in hard times.

Tenant farming was another occupation that drained all family resources. Large families were the norm, and all members worked the fields. Many farm owners would not hire as tenants those farmers who had few children. Some families went back and forth from mill town to tenant farm, but in general, there seems to have been a great antipathy among the farmers to life in a mill town. It was seen as dangerous for children and at best a last resort when all else failed. Mill workers, for their part, looked upon tenant farming as backbreaking labor with nothing to show for it in the end, and some young farm women preferred millwork for the cash earnings. The farm family as an economic unit was indeed on the wane. After 1900, every decade saw a decline in the number of small, independent farms in America.

THE NEEDLE TRADES

The clothing industry showed the same trends as the cotton textile industry. As the work was mechanized and industrialized out of the home, women followed and were present in high concentrations in the industry. This was also an industry that absorbed generations of immigrant labor from the successive waves of arrivals from Europe. In 1860 women made up 64 percent of the clothing industry. By 1900 their portion was only 47 percent. The industry had expanded, and many women were taken into the shops and factories. However, because of the influx of many immigrant men and the phasing out of home industry and sweatshops, the overall employment of women in the trade was reduced.

[7] Jennings Rhyne, *Some Southern Cotton Mill Workers and Their Villages* (Chapel Hill: University of North Carolina Press, 1930), pp. 83–86.

The needle trades lent themselves very well to subcontracting. A man would contract with a firm to deliver so many articles for a certain rate; this man would then give the garments to a group of workers who stitched them in a little loft shop or in an apartment and were paid by the piece. This kind of work was almost tailor-made for immigrant mothers who, not knowing English and bound by old-country traditions that frowned on women working outside the home, could only earn money if the work came to them. Sewing was a skill they already knew. However, they were subject to abuses that made the period the dark ages of industrial labor. Eventually, conditions led to a general outcry and to legislation banning sweated labor. Yet, as late as the 1930s, home industrial work, though under improved conditions, continued as a mode of production. In 1927 New York State reported over 21,500 persons engaged in industrial work at home in *licensed* houses. In New York City alone 1,467 employers gave industrial home work to 11,516 workers during the same year.[8] It is said that many Italian families weathered the depression years in New York State through the industrial home work of the women, which brought in income without disrupting the families and without making the men lose face by seeing their women leave home to find work.

Industry did not always have sources of cheap labor fall into its waiting lap. For example, soft industries such as the manufacture of silk, cigars, and boxes moved into coal and steel areas to get at the women in the steel-mill and coal-mining families. This deliberate move on the part of industry has been documented for Pennsylvania from the 1880s to the 1920s.

WHITE-COLLAR WORK

Throughout the nineteenth century, opportunities for women in nonfactory employment grew steadily. By the final decades of the century, all classes were at least represented in the female labor force, and four-fifths of these women were in nonfactory employment. Thousands of women had also been relieved of the necessity of earning a living. Their leisure was the most conspicuous social product of "the accumulations of the middle-classes, insurance schemes, new inheritance laws."[9]

[8]Emily C. Brown, *Industrial Home Work*, U.S. Women's Bureau, Department of Labor, Bulletin no. 79, 1930, p. 2
[9]Charles Beard and Mary R. Beard, *The Rise of American Civilization* (New York: Macmillan, 1930), 2: 721.

Women found openings in certain sectors of white-collar work. Of the professions, nursing and schoolteaching offered the path of least resistance to women. Mainly, however, women were drawn into the lower ranks of white-collar work as saleswomen, telephone and telegraph operators, and clerks and secretaries. The rapid development of industry and business created a network of operations in retailing, communications, and office work. Like the textile industry when it first recruited young women to the mills, telephone companies and business firms in the late nineteenth century wooed young women into jobs by projecting an image of decent, even interesting, work in proper surroundings. By 1900 there were over one million women working in various branches of white-collar work.

Class Distinctions   Early in the previous century, women and children became the most readily available labor source for emerging industries in a period when most of the men were required for farming. Passing mention has been made of the fact that there was not as yet any social stigma involved for middle-class young women who went to work in the factories prior to marriage. The class breakdown in women's employment had not yet materialized. However, by mid-century the class lines had been drawn, as a permanent body of wage-earning women entered the factories, increasingly of immigrant background, older, and more often married. As the cult of genteel womanhood took hold, fewer forms of employment became permissible for women aspiring to amount to something in society. And, increasingly, it was class that determined the views on women's proper roles: "A family had to have the means to support its women in sheltered idleness before it could come to believe that this was their natural state."[10]

It is not a coincidence that many of the women who wrote novels in the Victorian period came from families whose men had failed, because of either illness or bankruptcy to provide sufficient financial support. In those days, novel writing could be a lucrative profession, and in the face of the men's failure, the women went to work.

Because of their relative inactivity middle-class women, in many cases, were able to be given more formal education than their male relatives, who were ushered immediately into business. White-collar work, which began to materialize toward the end of the century, was

[10] Robert W. Smuts, *Women and Work in America* (New York: Columbia University Press, 1959), p. 137.

able to draw upon these unemployed, educated women. For these women such "proper" work represented the means of maintaining the family's foothold in the middle class without losing class in the process.

Reorganization of White-Collar Work   The old positions of clerk and secretary, when held by men, had been jobs requiring not a little responsibility and prestige; as such they were part of management. At the same time that women were entering the field, clerical work was being reorganized into more routine jobs at a fraction of the pay. Women, it was rationalized, were ideally suited to the work of keeping offices running because they had patience and nimble fingers and were not easily bored by repetitive tasks.

Around these female office workers a certain timeless fairy tale was fabricated. Again, the parallels to the romantic myths surrounding women mill operatives of Lowell are there. The secretary, it was thought around the turn of the century, was a pacesetter, a style-maker, and an all-around consumer.[11]

The typewriter was introduced to offices in the 1870s. In 1881 the Central Branch of the New York City YWCA offered a small class for women in typewriting. The YWCA was soon swamped with applications for such classes, and had to turn away scores of women. With the casual standards then prevailing in industrial training and even in professional fields, office stenographers and typists, thanks to classes such as these, had perhaps the best vocational training then offered working women.[12] By 1915 the typewriter was an accepted part of office machinery. Between 1910 and 1920 there was a jump in the number of white women in clerical and sales work.

The United States government officially recognized the growing importance of women in white-collar work by the passage in 1919 by the Civil Service Commission of a ruling opening all civil service exams to both men and women.

The stages in the development of office technology paralleled those we have already observed in regard to household technology. In each case the reorganization of the work preceded the arrival of the machinery. Office work had proliferated and been subdivided into separate jobs for several decades before, in the second decade of the century,

[11] Bruce Bliven, Jr., *The Wonderful Writing Machine* (New York: Random House, 1954), p. 8.
[12] Smuts, *Women and Work in America*, p. 83.

machines such as the typewriter and adding machine became widely used. Once mechanization was achieved, the logical step was centralization of operations to ensure the optimal utilization of the machinery. C. Wright Mills analyzes this process from reorganization to mechanization to centralization in his book *White Collar*.[13] In Mills's categories, by 1940 some 40 percent of white-collar workers in the new middle class were office workers, 25 percent were salespeople, 25 percent were salaried professionals, and only 10 percent were managers. Mills also found that some 41 percent of all white-collar workers were women, and that throughout the "white-collar pyramid" position was graded by age and sex.[14]

White-Collar Relationships During the 1950s, David Riesman and Mills, among others, called attention to the nature of relationships between managers and secretarial staff in the office. Riesman described the privatized lives of women office workers that drove them to seek personal satisfaction from their jobs. Since their work itself lacked the necessary significance, office workers looked for satisfaction "in the boss and in the super-structure of emotions they weave into the office situation."[15]

The "coercive friendliness" that pervades the office world then comes to infect the way white-collar workers relate to people away from work as well. What Riesman insufficiently emphasized was the extent to which these personalized relationships at work are forced upon white-collar workers. C. Wright Mills did this, referring to the "personality market," in which white-collar workers must sell not only their time, energy, and labor but their personalities as well. They must appear in the proper personalized manner toward all comers: consumer, client, or manager. How they relate to people becomes a commodity.[16] Mills quotes a passage from a Christopher Morley novel in which Kitty Foyle speaks of white-collar women like herself as "share-croppers, niggers in the field."

The public image of female white-collar workers, revolving around the attractive secretary, was an entirely different matter. The 1940s

[13] C. Wright Mills, *White Collar* (New York: Oxford University Press, 1956), pp. 192–196.
[14] *Ibid.*, pp. 74–75.
[15] David Riesman, Nathan Glazer, and Reuel Denney, *The Lonely Crowd* (New York: Doubleday, Anchor Books, 1950), pp. 304–305.
[16] Mills, *White Collar*, p. 182.

and 1950s was the period of Katharine Hepburn and Joan Crawford movies showing the glamorous lives of these "girls Friday." The same mentality produced statements that the secretary had the "average business office . . . under fairly good control" or that "American business is conducted at the pace the American secretary sets, or something between forty and seventy words per minute."[17]

The Assembly-Line Department   By 1956 white-collar occupations outnumbered blue-collar ones in the nation's economy. The white-collar sector had grown three and a half times faster than the entire labor force.[18] Ironically, as the white collar edged the blue collar out of the largest share of the labor market, white-collar work has taken on more of the attributes of blue-collar work. Many large white-collar departments are run on the assembly-line pattern. Papers are passed from worker to worker; no individual worker completes one entire report or compilation.[19] Such work is highly automated, and the noise of machines can make an office *sound* like an assembly line as well. No longer is one executive closeted away with several assistants and secretaries; the new white-collar enterprise is a highly organized mass operation with many women under the supervision of the counterpart to the factory foreman or forewoman. There are speedups and efforts to regiment workers' relationships by prohibiting conversations, smoking, etc. For example, one occupation that would seem to straddle the line between white- and blue-collar work—that of telephone operator—has always functioned under highly regimented and coercive working conditions. The Bell System has been castigated repeatedly by official committees for its labor abuses.

At the bottom of the white-collar "hierarchies," understandably, the turnover rate is quite high. Whereas personnel managers often bemoan the high turnover rate of their women workers in such jobs, there is conflicting evidence as to whether a high turnover rate is so disadvantageous for the businesses. One personnel manager in a large insurance company interviewed by C. Wright Mills's team stated that the high turnover rate was to the company's liking. The work required very little training, and continuity of staff was not important. The company preferred to hire young girls with at least two years of high

[17]Bliven, *Wonderful Writing Machine*, p. 5.
[18]Baker, *Technology and Woman's Work*, p. 335.
[19]L. Valmeras, "The Work Community," *Radical America* 5, no. 4 (July–August 1971): 77–92.

school in the semidependent or wholly dependent categories—living at home and contributing to family income. (Other companies find young women harder to handle and prefer older married women.) There is also some advantage for the workers, since those who stay on at jobs in high turnover categories have a good chance at promotion.

There are indications that the new white-collar working conditions are producing a new consciousness among the employees. The old office mentality that led secretaries and file clerks to give their loyalty to their boss now leads them to identify with their co-workers, with whom they spend so many hours every day and upon whose support and confidence they depend to keep some control over their jobs. As the gap widens between managerial and clerical staffs, the chances for a new solidarity among clerical workers increase. (We should note, however, that this has been the hope of certain groups within the labor movement for many decades.)

Professional Work   The one white-collar area in which women have not shared in the overall expansion has been professional work. In fact, there has been a decline—with minor fluctuations—in the percentage of women in professional jobs since 1930. Part of this decline may have been accentuated by the census categories prior to 1930, which tended to group under the label "professional" certain jobs that later were entered under a variety of different headings. From 1940 to 1968 the proportion of women in professional and technical fields declined from 45 percent to 39 percent. Whereas professional women often feel themselves to be in the vanguard of all working women—the wedge in the door of advancement and success—the statistics do not show this.

One of women's traditional strongholds within professional occupations has been teaching. In 1968 women were still 70 percent of all teachers, the highest proportion being in elementary teaching. Because of a concerted effort to recruit more men into high school teaching, the percentage of women in the field as a whole declined between 1950 and 1960. In higher education women tend to be concentrated in colleges—especially junior colleges—rather than in universities with graduate programs and emphasis on research. Here also women's participation declined from 23 percent to 19 percent between 1950 and 1960, a steady decrease since the 32 percent in 1930.

It is too early yet to predict with certainty what effect the drop in birthrate will have through the next generations on the schools of the country and hence on women's employment in them. However, perhaps a little speculation is in order: It is a fact that there is a higher proportion of unmarried women than unmarried men in the professions. Marriage seems to be a liability for women who might wish to enter professional fields. Furthermore, it has been established that wives of top professionals are less likely to work than the wives of those in the lower professional ranks.[20] Therefore, not only would a married professional woman have the burden of carrying a double work load—one in her field and one at home—but she would also be competing with male colleagues whose main female role models—their wives—would not be likely to fill the image of an independent working woman. Recent population reports indicate that there are a greater number of single young women than ever before; these young women may well opt for increased education and professional jobs in the future. In teaching this would mean increased competition between men and women for fewer positions, for the decreased birthrate—unless it is reversed soon—will mean fewer students at all ages and levels.

Conclusion

This chronicle of women's labor history shows how, over generations, women have made the adjustment from domestic production to work outside the home. As workers, women have been present at critical junctures in economic development—as factory operatives in the emerging industries and later as office workers in the seemingly endless expansion of the white-collar occupations.

This active labor history cuts straight through the Victorian era. The realities of work serve as a counterbalance to the myths and cults of womanhood that preoccupied the more leisured classes of that era.

The first half of the twentieth century has seen a consolidation of trends in the female work force that were, in essence, established in the previous century. The situation of women in the work force will continue to evolve; past patterns will guide the nature of the evolution and its interpretation.

[20]Cynthia Fuchs Epstein, *Woman's Place. Options and Limits in Professional Careers* (Berkeley: University of California Press, 1970), p. 116.

chapter 4

WOMEN AT WORK
ECONOMIC CRISIS, EMPLOYMENT PATTERNS, UNIONS

The history of the textile and related industries of the nineteenth century and the white-collar empires of the twentieth century shows that women have been present at epoch-making junctures of the American economy. However, their status, wages, and working conditions within these central occupations show little advancement in the course of time. As we examine in this chapter the significance of economic crisis, women's employment patterns, and the union movement, it will become clear that while female labor has served long and hard, the jobs requiring great skill or strength have been reserved for men.

Economic Crisis

TIMES OF WAR

One of the traditional theories in women's labor history is that wars are responsible for the progress in women's employment. In the past the most recent war often has been pointed to not only as the occasion but also as the most important reason for women's accelerated entry into the labor force.[1] The men were at war, the reasoning goes; therefore, women were called upon to take their places and were not found wanting. The experiences of management, industry, and women during the war *did* change social attitudes toward working women. However, as

[1] Oppenheimer, Valerie Kincade, *The Female Labor Force in the United States. Demographic and Economic Factors Governing Its Growth and Changing Composition* (Berkeley: Institute of International Studies, University of California, 1970).

has been noted, social attitudes on women and work have merged rather closely with prevailing economic directions.

The first war for which information is readily available on the employment of women is the Civil War. Women were, of course, also much occupied during the Revolutionary War, as we know from the letters of Abigail Adams and her contemporaries as well as from newspapers. However, as the most sweeping developments in women's labor history occurred in the nineteenth century, it is reasonable that the Civil War should have had a more pronounced effect upon women and the labor force.

More women actually fought in the infantry during the war than is suspected. Mary Livermore, who chronicled Union women's service during the war, wrote of several such women in uniform:

> *I remember Annie Etheridge, of Michigan, who was with the Third Michigan in every battle in which it was engaged . . . . Bridget Devens, known as "Michigan Bridget," went to the field with the First Michigan Cavalry, in which her husband was a private, and served through the war. Sometimes when a soldier fell she took his place, fighting in his stead with unquailing courage . . . .*[2]

More typically, women took jobs left vacant by men during the war—in farm work, factory work, and teaching. It was during the Civil War that nursing got its start as a profession with national organizations. Whereas the Civil War did not have quite the same boosting effect in regard to women and the labor force that World War II and, to a lesser degree, World War I had, the war seems to have occasioned a general expansion in communications networks, transportation, industry, education, and bureaucracy. The depression of the cotton industry during and immediately following the war had the effect of relocating women permanently, in many cases, in other forms of employment. The tremendous federal support given public education on all levels in this period also laid the groundwork for women's twentieth-century entrance into the white-collar world. Because of the economic devastation of the South, it would be several decades yet until white Southern women would be able to participate in any activity not connected with

---

[2] Mary A. Livermore, *My Story of the War* (Hartford: A. D. Worthington, 1892), p. 116.

regaining and securing economic stability. Indeed, the economic and social disruption that the war caused in the North and South can hardly be overemphasized.

World War I saw women entering war industries. Estimates are that over one million women were making war supplies. They also entered some previously all-male jobs becoming, for example, conductors on trains and streetcars. It was during this war that the forerunner of the U.S. Women's Bureau was set up within the Labor Department, initially to supervise the influx of women into war industries and to aid in setting up standards for the employment of women in industry. The Woman in Industry Service was sorry not to see the increase in women's industrial employment carry over into the postwar years. Numerous commentators have stressed the fact that the almost twenty months during which the United States was in the war were too short a time for women to overcome the barriers in a permanent way. Indeed, between 1910 and 1920 there was a 6 percent decrease in the number of white women in the "manual and service sector" and a 21 percent decrease in the number of black women in this sector. However, in the same decade there was a 103 percent increase of white women and a 122 percent increase of black women in the sector of "clerical and sales workers." The war had affected women's place in the labor force, but not in the way of giving women jobs formerly held by men. Rather, the war led to a renewed proliferation of office and sales work, which women had already established themselves in by the end of the previous century.

The military establishment for its part was intrigued by the possibilities that female labor power held for the waging of future wars. According to Major General Hanson E. Ely of the Army:

> Women will play a greater part in future wars. Governments, including our own, have been studying use of women in war. Women power will in some instances supplant and in other cases supplement man-power in the next war. Utilization of women will grow, in the final analysis, out of a new conception of warmaking, born during the last war. The struggle was so gigantic that, for the countries involved, war-making became the national industry.[3]

[3] From *The New York American,* April 8, 1931, as quoted in Grace Hutchins, *Women Who Work* (New York: International Publishers, 1934), pp. 33–34.

World War II, as was expected, increased the immediate need for female labor. Women were drawn heavily into both industry and farm work. The decade of the 1940s showed the overall change in distribution. There was a 100 percent increase in the employment of white women in industry, as opposed to the 4 percent increase during the decade of World War I. White females were the only group in the labor force that showed any percentage gain in the category of farm labor, with an increase of 76 percent. Black women made up for the meager gains in labor force participation in previous decades with a 138 percent increase in the white-collar sector, particularly in clerical and sales work, where the rise was 348 percent. There was a 334 percent increase in the number of black women working as skilled workers and foremen. During the war the number of women working for the federal government, doing primarily office work, rose from one-fifth to two-fifths of the total.

From 75 to 85 percent of women interviewed in one study done in 1944 and 1945 stated that they wished to continue working after the war ended.[4] In fact, many women were dropped from their jobs at the end of the war, lowering the number of women in the labor force from 20.3 million to 15.9 million between 1945 and 1947. After 1947 the increase of women in jobs continued at the pace set in the previous century. The end of the Vietnam War has not affected women's employment, just as the end of the Korean War was not followed by anything but the slightest drop in the employment of women.

ECONOMIC DEPRESSION

If wars bring on vigorous debates on women and the job world, the debates sparked by economic depression are even more intense. Each depression brings the accusation that women are taking jobs that men need. Actually, women are rarely in direct competition over the same jobs because of the well-established segregation of men's jobs and women's. It is true that there was sharp competition for jobs between men and women in some professional and technical fields. The unemployment rate for these women was high enough to alarm women's groups. The overall unemployment rate for women in 1931 was, however, lower than that of men: 26.2 percent of men as opposed to 18.9

---

[4] Women's Bureau Bulletin No. 209. U.S. Department of Labor, Government Printing Office, 1945.

percent of women workers were unemployed. Because so many fathers, brothers, and husbands were unemployed, many women were forced to find jobs for the first time between 1930 and 1940.

In times of normal ups and downs of the economy, women do have a consistently higher rate of unemployment than do men. Whereas women are under 40 percent of the labor force, they are over 50 percent of all unemployed workers. In 1968, there was 2.9 percent unemployment among men and 4.8 percent among women. In 1967, 4.5 percent of the women heads of families in the labor force were unemployed, as compared with the 2.1 percent unemployment among male family heads. Non-white women fared even worse, with 8.3 percent unemployment. These figures represent the penalities that women workers pay as a result of their precarious position in the labor force.

Employment Patterns

WOMEN'S WAGES

Industry and business have found women an attractive source of labor at certain periods because of their greater availability and cheapness. There were times when employers could not possibly have gotten male workers if they had wanted them; this labor situation plus the perennial availability and cheapness of female labor overcame whatever prejudices against hiring women might have existed in industry or business.

The pattern for the celebrated cheapness of female labor was set by the position of women in the family as it had evolved by the early nineteenth century. By then women were fast losing their productive capacity within the family and thus their economic independence. The supportive and subsidiary roles they had assumed in relation to men in the family—while yet performing indispensably within the family economy—had affected position of women in all classes. It was thus that the public and the women themselves could be persuaded by industry that any occupation should be welcomed that took these idle and dependent women and allowed them to cease being an economic drain upon family resources and instead to contribute in some modest way. The temporary floor set to women's industrial wages by the competing demands upon labor of a land-rich society had passed by mid-century. And forever after, women have regularly and blatantly received less pay than men.

The classic views on why women have had no claim on higher wages in whatever occupations they found themselves are briefly these: women are inefficient, physically weak, submissive, often sick; they work on nonessential products and are lacking in skill, resourcefulness, initiative, and organizational ability; they eat less and therefore need less money; their earnings are supplemented by those of their husbands, or by allowances from parents; single women are only working until they can marry; *and*, furthermore, if women were paid more, more of them would be tempted to leave home and compete with men for jobs.[5]

Actually, in real labor situations, men have not had to call upon these fallacious reasons very often, for it is not often that men and women actually do the same work, thus providing situations where such comparisons in wages would arise. The differentiation and discrimination against women begins earlier in the division of jobs. The thrust for equal pay for equal work becomes quite blunted if there is no equal work to begin with.

MEN'S WORK, WOMEN'S WORK

The way in which certain jobs became known as men's work and others as women's work is a story in itself. One of the most striking features of women's labor history is the longevity of these sex divisions of jobs. As mentioned above, the general rule of thumb has been that men get the better jobs. Even within ethnic and racial groups, the same sex-based hierarchy prevails, with the black woman on the bottom.

In general, women have been concentrated in those industries manufacturing nondurable products and in those nonindustrial occupations involving what could be interpreted as "service"—domestic work, nursing, teaching, office work. These major breakdowns could be a carryover from female roles in the family, which tended to put upon the woman the major burden of serving the family's needs and of making food and other articles to be "consumed" by the family. However, within a given industry, jobs have been assigned to males or females on often totally arbitrary grounds. Indeed, it often seems that a job receives a higher rating in skill and status simply because men are employed in it.

---

[5] Frank H. Streightoff, *The Standard of Living Among the Industrial People of America* (Boston: Hart, Schaffner and Marx Prize Essays, 1911).

TECHNOLOGICAL INNOVATION

Technology has played an uneven function in regard to women's distribution in industrial occupations. New machinery and production processes that changed the "physical and skill requirements" of work have led to the employment of women in some industries formerly restricted to men. Male craftsmen became obsolete as women were hired to do what amounted to semiskilled assembly-line work. This was the case in the making of watches and clocks; in the period from the mid-1800s to 1900, women in occupations in the classification "metals and metal products other than iron and steel" rose from less than 1,000 to over 25,000.[6]

Nevertheless, women did best in those industries in which they had been a major part from the beginning or close to it. Moreover, technological innovations were not unfailingly the occasion for women's admittance into an industry. The powerful union in the printing industry acted quickly to forestall entry of women following the introduction of Linotype machines, which automated the work of typesetters. The union accomplished this by stipulating that the new machines be operated only by "journeymen printers trained in the trade as a whole."[7] There were no women who fit this category; therefore, the men had their way. Automation also failed to work to women's advantage in the telephone industry. There automation hit the number of jobs at the switchboard but left relatively unaffected jobs that men hold in the industry.[8]

PROFESSIONALIZATION

From the latter half of the eighteenth century women had felt the disadvantages of being excluded from much of the specialized training necessary in some professions and trades. Previously women had been found acting as attorneys, pharmacists, and doctors in the days when what was needed was a certain knack, a competence, and simply the faculty of being in the right place at the right time. In the eighteenth

[6] Elizabeth Faulkner Baker, *Technology and Woman's Work* (New York: Columbia University Press, 1964), pp. 49–50.
[7] *Ibid.*, p. 44.
[8] Ernest R. Groves, *The American Woman* (New York: Emerson Books, 1944), pp. 336–337.

and nineteenth centuries, women lost substantial ground in the medical field, particularly in the area of midwifery. From colonial times, midwives had held a highly respected position in communities. During the nineteenth century midwives found themselves relegated to rural communities only, as the "accoucheurs" with their new "obstetrics" took over the profession. It was very difficult if not impossible for women to acquire the necessary higher education in what passed for medical studies in those days; the new obstetricians were men. Ironically, therefore, women were deprived of female medical attention in childbirth precisely during the period when Victorian mores prescribed an excessively modest, even shameful, attitude toward the female body. To this day, men dominate the field of obstetrics and gynecology. Thus, the professionalization of skills acted to erase women's traditional status in medicine, as in other fields of endeavor.

EMPLOYMENT OF MINORITIES

The employment of ethnic and racial minorities has mirrored in many details the patterns characteristic of women's labor history. Although throughout the industrial period native-born white women have remained better represented in the more lucrative and skilled jobs than nonwhite men and women and certain white ethnic minorities, the competition among these groups has been bitter. As waves of immigration brought new supplies of cheap labor into this country, women, unskilled male workers, blacks, Mexicans, Japanese, Chinese, Russians, Italians, and others have supplanted one another at the bottom of the occupational ranks. Instances of labor solidarity have been recorded among these groups, but they have been rare. The labor union movement, for example, has yet to organize these groups across their sex, racial, and ethnic lines.

Unions

UNION MEMBERSHIP

Unions are central to the dilemmas of women's position in the labor force. As of 1968, 3.7 million union members, or 19.5 percent of the total membership, were women. This is a 1.3 percent increase since 1958. However, the percentage of all women workers who are unionized has actually decreased during the 1958–1968 period from 13.8 percent to 12.5 percent. Women are not evenly distributed among unions; three-quarters of all women union members are concentrated in twenty-one unions. The tendency is for women to be better represented in the unaffiliated unions. It is thought that this may be a function of the fact that unaffiliated unions are found in the service industries and in communications and the electrical machinery trades, where women are in a high percentage.

The major areas of gain in union membership of women have reflected the trend of their concentration in the white-collar and service occupations. For example, one-fourth of the 600,000-member gain in female union membership between 1958 and 1968 was in four unions alone: Retail Clerks International, Service Employees International, United Automobile Workers, and the American Federation of Government Employees. And yet, no one claims that unions have done more than skim the surface in reaching women workers.

Many of the causes for women's marginal representation in this country's trade unions are rooted in the origins and directions of the labor movement. We cannot attempt here any sort of total critique of that movement, but we can point to certain episodes in that history, as they bear on the problems facing women and unions.

WOMEN AND THE LABOR MOVEMENT

Women have a history of encounters with unions dating back to the 1820s, the early period of industrial expansion. It is a frustrating history filled with many skirmishes with management and with male unionists, some major landmark strikes, and the almost continual refusal of the union leadership to give consistent aid to the women in their struggles.

Not surprisingly, the bulk of women's trade union experience during the previous century centered in the textile and garment trades. Given the highly paternalistic conditions at the New England mills, it is not surprising that organized activity among the female mill hands took some time to develop momentum. In 1826, when some 66,000 women were in the mills, some of the first men's unions of carpenters, printers, and shoemakers were founded. In 1828 there was a turnout of 300 to 400 women at the Cocheco Company mill in Dover, New Hampshire, over "restrictive regulations." All over New England there were similar uprisings. Lowell, Massachusetts, saw several impressive strikes. In 1834 some 800 women walked out and withdrew their savings from the town bank, made statements that were picked up by the press that "union is power," and announced a series of strike resolutions. There was some contact between the striking women of several mills. The Lowell strike of 1836, with up to 2,500 striking, was the largest and longest ever held up to that time in the mills. The marching strikers sang the now famous lines: "Oh, isn't it a pity, such a pretty girl as I/Should be sent into the factory to pine away and die." The immediate issue—an increase in room-and-board pay deductions—soon was expanded into a program of resolutions. Out of this strike the Factory Girls' Association was formed, and it drew a resolution of sympathy for the striking women from the third annual convention of the National Trades Union, meeting then in Philadelphia. At the same convention the NTU heard a report from its Committee on Female Labor castigating women mill operatives for not building *permanent* societies for mutual aid.[9]

Toward mid-century, the Lowell Female Labor Association was formed under the leadership of mill hand Sarah Bagley. The Association had branches in many other cities and was a real trade union (the name notwithstanding), drawing its membership from local working women.[10] These associations failed to produce a strong union of women. The reasons are the classic ones: faced with low pay, long hours, and oppressive conditions, too many women, rather than seek changes, decided simply to endure the hardships for the relatively few years they would be involved in factory work. They could see, of course, that their labor was being exploited; the twelve- or thirteen-hour day was long. Yet, many were unwilling to work less and thereby lose the extra pay. On the other side, these early women's unions were stunted by a lack of resources, since so much time, money, and energy was being absorbed by the mills. With no concrete help coming in from fraternal unions, the associations faded away.

Throughout the 1850s and 1860s, trade union activity among women was sporadic and local in nature. Finally, in 1869 the first national women's union was formed in the boot and shoe industry—Daughters of Saint Crispin—affiliated with the Knights of Saint Crispin. The National Labour Union, one of the pioneer trade union federations, had in 1865 resolved to give higher priority to women workers in the future.

[9]Hannah Josephson, *Golden Threads* (New York: Duell, Sloan and Pearce, 1949), pp. 238–239.
[10]Alice Henry, *The Trade Union Woman* (New York: D. Appleton, 1915), pp. 12–13.

However, of the thirty or so national unions in the 1860s and 1870s, only a few even admitted women. Among that handful admitting women were the printers—and thereby hangs a tale.

The printers had been very antiwoman at mid-century. The printers had been particularly adamant that the women, whom they perceived only as strike breakers, should not enter their field. In 1856 the Boston Typographical Union vented its animosity in this way:

> Resolved, *That this society discountenances any member working in any office that employs female compositors, and that any member found doing so be discharged from the society.*[11]

The printers were obliged to retract this statement a short while later, as women continued to enter the trade. Denying that it had ever "discountenanced" the employment of women compositors, the union urged women to organize among themselves to keep their wages up.

The Women's Typographical Union Local No. 1 was founded in 1868, but went out of existence in 1878. The local met with the recalcitrance of union men and the repressive tactics of the employers, who systematically laid off women who were suspected of union organizing. The bitterness of the report submitted by Augusta Lewis to the 1871 union convention reveals the true attitude of union men toward their sisters: "It is the general opinion of female compositors that they are more justly treated by what is termed 'rat' foremen, printers and employers than they are by union men."[12]

There were few, if any, other women's locals in the period. Women continued to participate loyally in the strikes and agitations of the male-dominated unions and to receive in return little support from the men in those unions.

In 1875, at a meeting from which all men except reporters had been barred, a group of women weavers voted to strike. The men weavers had previously voted to accept a reduction in wages at a meeting without women. In the end the men joined the women in the strike. Although in this case, the result was a joint action, women did not often fare so well. Historian Eleanor Flexner concludes that the women

[11] Edith Abbott, *Women in Industry* (New York: D. Appleton, 1910), p. 252.
[12] Eleanor Flexner, *Century of Struggle* (New York: Atheneum, 1970), pp. 134–137.

during this period were at a great disadvantage, having to work within locals dominated by men and without strong support from the leadership. Their subsidiary position made it impossible for them to develop their own leaders and to give priority to the particular problems affecting women in the trades.[13]

The peak of the labor militance among women in industry came in the garment trades in the second decade of the twentieth century; however, women had been organized in these trades since the closing decades of the nineteenth century. In San Francisco, late in the last century, women were able to form a militant and successful local despite the distractions in the union stemming from anti-Chinese feeling. There was one incident in particular that shows that women did not always share the racist views of their union brothers. Union publications had been bemoaning the fact that white female garment workers sometimes had to work alongside Chinese male workers or under Chinese foremen. Therefore, there was quite a bit of amazement when, in 1890, a group of white women reported that they preferred working in the Chinese garment factory because they were satisfied with conditions and because the Chinese did not insult them as white men did. The reporter covering this incident could explain the choice of the women only on the ground that they were so desperate they would accept employment wherever they could get it.[14]

Women in the San Francisco garment industry went on to take control of Local No. 131 of the United Garment Workers, founded in 1900. The women voted the men out of the local and had complete control over the affairs of the union. The women in the garment workers' union were reportedly the most active and able of all union women in the San Francisco area, not only in their own interests but in those of the general labor movement as well.

In spite of all this union activity, union membership for women around 1910 was estimated at only 1.5 percent of all female wage earners.[15] However, in the garment trades in New York City union membership took a quick upward surge. This increase was reflected in the state as a whole; between 1908 and 1913 the number of unionized women in New York State rose from 10,698 to 78,522.[16]

[13] Ibid., p. 137.
[14] Lillian R. Matthews, "Women in Trade Unions in San Francisco," University of California in Economics 3, no. 1 (1913): 9.
[15] Flexner, Century of Struggle, p. 246.
[16] Henry, Trade Union Woman, p. 41.

The garment industry had by 1909 made the changeover from tenement sweatshops to factory lofts. The unions, which had temporarily been thwarted by the new conditions, had by 1909 a new generation of women working in the garment trades. These young women, many of them Russian Jews, had come to this country with a heritage of political struggle. For them it was no shame to organize to protect their rights. Previously, the split between the Italian immigrant women and the Russian Jewish women had proved one of the most difficult obstacles to union work in the garment trades. In November 1909, internal tensions combined with generalized discontent over working conditions to produce the Uprising of the Twenty Thousand. The industry was 80 percent women, and 75 percent of the strikers were women between the ages of sixteen and twenty-five. More spectacularly, it was the first general strike in the industry, with more than five hundred shops closed.[17] Hundreds of women were jailed in the picketing and demonstrations that followed, and the strike lasted until February 15, 1910.

Although the strike ended in settlements shop by shop, which weakened the impact of the union demands, for the labor movement and for women workers the strike became an event cherished as a triumph. The strike had proved that women could organize, could undergo the test of a long strike, picket lines, arrests; and it had further proved that the dual obstacles of ethnic differences and the supposedly submissive nature of women could be overcome. In still larger terms, the strike dramatized the deplorable conditions of the sweatshops. (Little more than a year later, on March 25, 1911, the fire that gutted the Triangle Waist Company's factory, claiming the lives of over 100 women, was to show any who still needed convincing the murderous contempt industry had for labor.)

The official chronicler for the Garment Workers Union has in effect underplayed the significance of the shirtwaist makers' strike, calling it a prologue to the more important cloakmakers' strike that followed in 1910. This strike involved more men workers, as not many women were then in that industry. It was a larger strike and spread to several cities. (It would be interesting to speculate on the respective evaluation that would be given the two strikes if the order had been reversed. Most likely the men, in striking first locally, would have claimed they had shown the women how it was done.)

[17]Louis Levine, *The Women's Garment Workers Union: A History of the International Ladies' Garment Workers Union* (New York: B. W. Huebsch, 1924), p. 144; Ronald Sander, *The Downtown Jews* (New York: Harper and Row, 1969), pp. 398–399.

An important variable brought up by the official International Ladies Garment Workers Union report was the participation in the women's strike of groups outside the union circles proper. It is true that the Women's Trade Union League and some suffragist groups had a hand in some of the day-to-day efforts during the strike months. For some unionists the sight of wealthy suffragists renting halls for strike meetings spoiled the picture of independent women workers striking on their own power. This complex relationship between the woman movement and the labor movement will be discussed in the next chapter.

ATTITUDES OF ORGANIZED LABOR

The attitude of organized labor to women workers can hardly be over-estimated as a curb on the participation of women in union activity. For a long time the organization of women within the labor movement meant to union officials nothing more than ladies' auxiliaries, for the female relatives of working men. The problem of women and trade unions goes deeper than just an inability of male unionists to take their laboring sisters seriously as workers. Male unionists have often fought the entry of women into their ranks and barred them from joining the unions. The men feared that the presence of women in their trade would bring down standards in wages and benefits and drive out the men. They feared this even as they barred women from the one kind of organization that might have allowed an across-the-board effort to strengthen the position of all workers.

In many instances the attitude of unions toward women parallels the attitude of craft unions toward unskilled or semiskilled labor in general. Where unions have relented and allowed women in, they have acted largely from motives of self-defense, rather than from an acknowledgment of a community of workers with common problems. This self-serving attitude of male unionists has been recorded by countless working women as well as outside observers. And it has infected the unions' approach toward the weakest links throughout the entire labor movement. In the laundry industry in San Francisco, union men tried within the space of a few decades to exclude both Japanese and women from their ranks. Whether it was an Anti-Jap Laundry League or resolutions barring women from union membership, the response of the unions to the exploitative practices of employers has been to hoard for the white, male skilled workers whatever concessions they could gain.

The record of the national labor organizations is little better when it comes to women. Even the Knights of Labor, which professed to recognize the unskilled as well as the skilled laborer as worthy of organization—even they were slow to recognize the rights of working women. In 1878 they finally adopted a clause in their program supporting equal pay for equal work for both sexes. Women were admitted on an equal basis into the Knights of Labor in 1881, and by 1886 there were about two hundred local assemblies composed entirely of women.

Yet from 1890 on, women's membership dwindled. The new national organization—the American Federation of Labor—did not do anything to alter the near absence of national organization in those trades with a high concentration of women. Generally union men agreed with employers on the position of women, believing women could get along on less, had little real labor value, and so forth. Even after the explosive spurts in labor agitation and the strikes involving women in the early 1900s, the Federation was reluctant to go beyond the passage of fraternal resolutions supporting the rights of women workers. The 1918 convention rejected a motion to amend the Federation's constitution to require the election of two women to the Executive Council.

Unions in the garment trades could not afford to ignore women, for women constituted an overwhelming majority of the workers in these industries. The Ladies Garment Workers Union and the Amalgamated Clothing Workers Union, among others, made a concerted effort to organize women. Today women are from 75 to 80 percent of the membership (but not of the leadership) of these unions.[18]

WHITE-COLLAR WORKERS

White-collar workers remain the largest single occupational group of workers outside the labor unions. At the upper levels, schoolteachers, social workers, nurses, and librarians have joined together in unions; however, in too many cases, under the guise of professionalism, such organizations have had a way of identifying more with management than with labor. There are, of course, differences among the unions. The American Federation of Teachers is a real union with a long and occasionally militant history, in contrast to the conservative National Education Association, which includes in its membership principals and school superintendents. Social workers have better collective bargaining provisions in their unions than do librarians and nurses, who remain almost unreached by organized labor. Telephone workers are

[18] Baker, *Technology and Woman's Work*, pp. 154–155.

organized but have the lowest standards in wages and conditions of all unionized white-collar workers. Salespeople have the largest proportion of white-collar workers unionized. Office workers have very weak union representation. Furthermore, office workers are being organized by so many different unions that concerted efforts are difficult.

Elise Diehl organized the first union of Stenographers and Type-writers (the original term for typists) in 1904 as Local No. 11655, AFL. Since then office workers have been organized by white-collar, industrial, and independent unions. This has created some competion. There will probably continue to be a contest between the white-collar unions and the industrial unions for control over the white-collar field. The United Automobile Workers, the United Steelworkers, the Teamsters, and others have made inroads among white-collar workers. As the white-collar sector grows and is increasingly "proletarianized," the emphasis on unionization of office workers of all sorts will increase.

THE FUTURE FOR WOMEN AND UNIONS

Women have not always been prime candidates for unionization. It is said that, in the past, the groups with the highest potential for labor organizing were permanent wage-earning groups working in skilled occupations and holding strategic positions in industries that themselves occupied key positions in the entire industrial scheme. Also important was the use of the right organizational tactics for the particular industry in question.[19] Women have too often been temporary workers in low-skill trades. Although their long service has made possible technical and commercial expansion, women have nonetheless been judged as occupying the marginal, nonessential ranks of labor. On all these counts, therefore, women would appear to be low-potential candidates for union organization. Additionally, another explanation offered for women's lack of enthusiasm for union work has been their tender age; however, the increasing maturity of most women workers has altered that picture.

Recent conventions held by the United Auto Workers, American Federation of Teachers, American Newspaper Guild, and the AFL–CIO have seen women raising the issues that face women in society and in unions. Women have raised anew their demands for day care centers and

[19] Theresa Wolfson, *The Woman Worker and the Trade Unions* (New York: International Publishers, 1926), p. 90.

for equality in opportunity, seniority rights, pay, and chances for promotion. Where they have not received satisfaction in regard to seniority, lay offs, pay, promotions, and transfers, many women have appealed directly to the Equal Employment Opportunity Commission for redress; in some cases violations were discovered, and both union and company have been ordered to rectify the situation.[20]

There is really no one within the union bureaucracies whom female labor organizers can turn to for advice and experience in building a strong union movement among women. Even if male unionists were not reluctant to give such assistance, the fact would remain that they most likely do not understand the unique problems of women workers. The pressures on and off the job for women, the expectations, self-definitions, and popular definitions they bring to their work have never been delved into beyond the most superficial levels.

It is hard to see what it is that working men would really stand to lose by fully accepting women as fellow workers. A truly united labor force might be able to organize effective general strikes and offer more comprehensive improvements in the lives of working people. (One can, of course, see how union officialdom, grown set in its ways of negotiating and exchanging piecemeal concessions with management, would balk at a union movement united across sex lines, with white-collar and industrial sectors joined together.)

It would be gratifying to point to philosophical reasons for women's lack of success in union organizing. The very existence of unions is, it would seem, predicated on a negative, resigned attitude toward work. Work is alienated; the job of unions is to get more pay for *less* work, not to get better and more liberating and creative work for more people. It would be nice to conclude that women, in not joining or forming unions, have shown their rejection of the mentality of working men who take pride in holding down jobs of no intrinsic value. However, the much more immediate and honest reason for women's low rate of union membership is the lack of opportunity due to the absence of unions for women and the lack of interest due to women's greater preoccupation with responsibilities for home and family.

More is necessary to solve the problems of the work world than simply the full and equal participation of women on the job and in unions. As has been pointed out, there are more mature women working

[20]Lucretia M. Dewey, "Women in Labor Unions," *Monthly Labor Review* 94, no. 2 (February 1971): 47.

now at paid jobs than ever before; these women may become more open to union organization because of their concern for promotions, seniority, pensions, and other benefits but they may also become less open to broader political organization. Once fully integrated into the man's world of the job, women, like men, may be less able to see beyond the immediate bread-and-butter issues.

Conclusion

By all objective standards, women have proven themselves as workers. They have put in long years of faithful service and shown skill, flexibility, and commitment. When given a fighting chance, women have formed and joined unions and taken risks. However, even today, when most women work at jobs at some point in their lives and many women work more or less steadily through their mature years, working women find the labor force to be alien territory. The attitudes and actions of unions, employers, and society combine to deny the validity of generations of women's labor force.

Some women have learned the tricks of the trade and are successful in functioning in male-dominated occupations. However, for the most part, women in the labor force have developed tactics for survival that are a combination of tenacity and resignation. It takes tenacity for women to stick it out in jobs where they are not wanted by the unions and are exploited by employers. It takes tenacity to accomplish the juggling act of managing job and home responsibilities on one's own. And that is also where the discipline of resignation enters in. Where personal security and happiness, the welfare of children and other dependents are jeopardized, women resign themselves to the practicable and the inevitable. They accept low-paying, part-time jobs when they must, but when opportunities for better work open up, they once again reshuffle baby-sitting and housework.

All the while many women continue a delicate but persistent campaign at home to create a looser division of labor among family members. Yet, the world of the job is rarely creative or rewarding enough to cause women to contemplate seriously giving up the peculiar mixture of privilege and penalty involved in being first and foremost wives and mothers. The privilege and penalty of being a woman are to be found even in life-styles which do not include children and in which marriage is replaced by one or a series of relatively lasting relationships. Men, of course, also face multiple pressures at work and at home and must respond and react according to the situation; moreover, men are also controlled by popular definitions of masculine behavior, as are women by definitions of femininity. However, the stress has been greater on women, who are being drawn out of the home to a greater extent than men are being drawn back into it.

As people reevaluate their priorities for work, home, and marriage, and as these institutions undergo further change, women may change their views on how best to find security, fulfillment, and happiness. The labor movement hopes for a new collective spirit among women workers. The current women's movement hopes for a collective spirit among housewives as well, emerging from the isolation of the home and transforming the world of work and play in the process.

part 3

THE WOMAN MOVEMENT

chapter 5

Origins of Rebellion

Woman movement is just one of the several names designating the grand momentum for the liberation of some groups of women that stretched from the early nineteenth century through the early twentieth century. There were also other designations: feminist movement, woman's rights movement, or suffrage movement. Some have felt that these terms were mutually exclusive, representing basic ideological splits. The particular term chosen for this chapter will be *woman movement* because that name was used up through the early twentieth century to imply the whole trend toward bettering women's condition.

Defining "woman movement" will be problematical. The feminist movement of the nineteenth century, which is said to have culminated in the granting of female suffrage in 1920, was actually far broader than the roster of national and state suffrage organizations. Even the context of contemporary political movements is not sufficient to give a satisfying view of these surges of women's rebellion. Therefore, while women's organizations must be examined, this examination must not become totally divorced from an investigation of the individual, spontaneous forms of resistance and protest that supplied the impetus for much of the organized activity.

It is hard to learn a great deal about women because so much of their lives is experienced anonymously and viewed through the distorting prisms of sex and class. To be sure, there have always been women who led public lives, and the story of their organizations and their public stances tells much about the condition of all women, and about politically conscious women in particular. However, movements of women have always had a select, not a mass, membership, and the mere existence of organizations does not prove the presence of social change. In this chapter if the brevity of our treatment of women's underground rebellion reflects the limitations imposed by the nature of this short history, it is also the measure of the work yet to be done in knowing women.

Early Rebels

Although the woman's movement reached its peak during the nineteenth century, which witnessed the greatest changes in women's social and economic position, instances of rebellion and intellectual controversy involving women had been present from America's beginnings. Margaret Brent made an unsuccessful but imposing bid for the vote in Maryland in the middle of the seventeenth century. Persecution of women in the name of God was rife during that century. The trial and banishment of Anne Hutchinson from the Massachusetts Bay Colony in the late 1630s foreshadowed the attempts to suppress the Quakers and the witch-hunts of Salem. Anne Hutchinson's lectures, which preached of a more kindly God than did the church fathers of Boston, reached beyond her circle of housewives to include their husbands, some of them prominent figures in the colony. Her heretical theology and her manner of disseminating it, represented, since she was a woman, a political act close to treason.

The first hanging for witchcraft occurred in 1648 and the last in 1692; in all, somewhere between thirty and forty women and men died, although many more were so accused but acquitted. Women were much more heavily implicated in the witch-hunt than were men. Many of the victims were unpopular personalities, but all too often those suspected were women whose skill in making medicines and treating illness exposed them to charges of brewing witches' potions and casting spells. It seems as if the woman who distinguished herself in any way—through beauty, ugliness, intelligence, skill, charm, or unpleasantness—ran the greatest risk of condemnation. The fact that the extent of the killing was more moderate than that in similar rampages in Europe does not detract from the terror.

It is hard to guess the effect upon women of the public condemnation and execution of other members of their sex, victims of the church state. Would the diaries of women of the time show that they inwardly rejected the view propounded by their men that to be a man and a religious rebel was wicked but to be a woman in the same standing was evil and demonic? Margaret Winthrop, wife of Governor John Winthrop, Anne Hutchinson's chief prosecutor, did not mention Anne Hutchinson by name but did record her own despair and doubts in her diary.

In the Puritan colonies of seventeenth-century New England, for women to form religious bodies or radical sects was regarded as an act with grave political consequences. Although the courageousness and sacrifice of these women did increase the freedom to establish new religious denominations, it is hard to locate actual changes they brought about in the lives of women within the established churches and in everyday life. The contribution of these women martyrs and rebels *was* outstanding as a source of inspiration to later generations of active women.

Women did band together to do good works during the eighteenth century. In New York a New York Ladies' Society for the Relief of Poor Widows with Small Children existed in 1797. In 1800 Boston had the Boston Female Asylum, and similar institutions were founded in Baltimore, Philadelphia, Providence, Salem, Troy, and Albany. In many of these, indigent girls and women were trained as domestic servants and then hired out to private homes. A history of women in the eighteenth century concludes: "There was some gain in having women organized for any purpose but the influence of these societies was on the whole conservative."[1] A scattering of women during this period also ran convent schools for girls, but in general through the eighteenth and well into the nineteenth century there was very little approval of organizations of women not expressly religious or charitable in nature.[2]

The whole period encompassing the years of the America's revolution and early nationhood was filled with questioning on the position of women. Mercy Warren was one of the first woman writers who publicly defended the female sex and its rights. John and Abigail Adams recognized the needs and contribution of women in many spheres of life, although John in particular, and probably Abigail as well, would have stopped short of actual suffrage for women. Their son John Quincy supported the right of women to petition their government during the abolition struggle in the 1830s. Another young

[1] Mary S. Benson, *Women in Eighteenth-Century America* (New York: Columbia University Press, 1935), pp. 178–179.
[2] Jennie C. Croly, *The History of the Woman's Club Movement in America* (New York: H. G. Allen, 1898), p. 9.

aspiring politician, Abraham Lincoln, running for office in Illinois in 1836, made the following pledge in a campaign statement that, interestingly enough, mentions women but not blacks:

> . . . I go for all sharing the privileges of the government who assist in bearing its burdens. Consequently, I go for admitting all whites to the rights of suffrage who pay taxes or bear arms (by no means excluding females).[3]

Despite all the opinions of notable Americans on the position of women, little or no improvement resulted. However, in the years to come these testimonials as to women's worth and women's grievances would be drawn upon by the women launching the woman movement.

The Abolition Movement

Women were heavily involved in all the agitation and discussion of the pre-Civil War period. Slave women were fighting for their survial and shepherding their families out of slavery. In the North, free black women were speaking up on behalf of their people. The women mill workers of New England were, as has been shown in the previous chapter, proving that their gentility could give way to a nascent class consciousness. However, the mounting momentum of the antislavery movement was the pivot of debate on women's issues in the 1830s and 1840s. The temperance movement was beginning to become active but would not reach its peak until the latter half of the century.

Because of the strong taboo on public speaking by women, most women who worked in or around the emerging abolition movement did so in women's discussion and reading circles or behind the scenes. However, three women in particular stand out in the histories of the period as having broken the silence of women in public—Frances Wright, and Sarah and Angelina Grimké.

FRANCES WRIGHT

Frances Wright, a British reformer, made several lecture tours in the United States between 1818 and 1836. She not only advocated radical

[3]*Sangamon Journal,* June 13, 1836, as quoted in A. G. Violette, *Economic Feminism in American Literature Prior to 1848,* University of Maine Studies, 2d ser., no. 2 (Orono, Me., 1925), p. 53.

changes in the legal position of women but also a whole range of women's natural rights, from education to sexuality. She was active in the antislavery movement. In her short-lived communal settlement in the backwoods of Kentucky, she tried to bring the races and the sexes together to build new ways for them to relate to one another beyond the confines of master-slave, husband-wife. All of her work earned her a reputation for eccentricity and made "Fanny Wrightism" synonymous with free love. She was too utopian and profoundly radical for most of her contemporaries, although societies organized in her name later went on to bring about some legislative reforms in New York State.

THE GRIMKÉ SISTERS

Sarah and Angelina Grimké were much more in the mainstream of American reform politics than Frances Wright, although they had to brave much of the same kind of public abuse and condemnation for their work.

The experience of the Grimké sisters during 1837 and 1838 discourages the idea that the relationship between the abolition movement and the woman movement was a mutually supportive one. The Grimkés and the other women who began in the abolition movement and went on to the woman movement were not aided by their brothers in the former cause when it came to their consciousness of the wrongs committed against womankind. On the contrary, the debate over the propriety and expedience of women's public participation in the antislavery fight nearly split the movement wide open. The opposition to the Grimkés was first raised, it is true, by some conservative clergymen outside the Anti-Slavery Society, yet the reactions within the Society to the challenge were very revealing.

There were conservatives in the antislavery camp who used many of the same biblical arguments against women that the proslavery side used to prove divine support for the institution of slavery.[4] There were moderates, such as Theodore Weld, Angelina's future husband, who worried that a public furor over the woman question would jeopardize support for the primary cause—antislavery. Their advice to the sisters was to continue their work for the slave but *not* to speak out or write specifically on woman's rights. Positive support for the women came

---

[4] Aileen S. Kraditor, *Means and Ends in American Abolitionism* (New York: Vintage Books, 1970), p. 44.

87

from the small group that felt that all impulses toward human liberation helped one another and that to remain silent when woman's rights
were challenged would be to blunt the potential of the antislavery
movement.[5]

The Grimkés made the decision not only to continue their work but
to stress woman's rights through a series of articles, to be written by
Sarah, that would range beyond their role in the antislavery movement.
Their initial reaction to the unexpected confrontation with the women's
cause is stated by Angelina as follows:

> I cannot help feeling some regret that this sh'ld come up
> before the Anti Slavery question was settled, so fearful am
> I that it may injure that blessed cause, and then again I
> think this must be the Lord's time and therefore the best
> time, for it seems to have been brought about by a con-
> catenation of circumstances over which we had no control.[6]

Just a few days later Angelina was insisting that "the time to assert a
right is *the* time when *that* right is denied.[7] And by October of 1837
she had progressed so far as to wonder "whether woman's rights are
not the *root*—whether they do not *lie deeper* than the rights involved
in our great question."[8]

It is obvious that the opposition the Grimkés encountered both outside and within abolition ranks deepened their understanding of oppression as it weighed on slaves and on women. Angelina wrote that both
women and freed slaves must feel a similar moral outrage when attentions were not paid them as a right but granted as a bounty.

However, the sisters retired from the movement in 1838 after
Angelina's marriage to Weld, Sarah joining her sister's new household.
This had not been their plan; they had hoped to prove that women
could both appear as public lecturers and still perform their domestic
duties. Angelina in particular had been hurt by the accusations of some
of her abolitionist brethren that she would not make a man a fit wife
after she had so overstepped the bounds of decorum. Her correspondence

---

[5] *Ibid.*, pp, 59–60.
[6] A. E. Grimké to T. Weld, August 12, 1837, *The Letters of Theodore Weld,
Angelina Grimké Weld and Sarah Grimké, 1822–1844,* edited by Gilbert H.
Barnes and Dwight L. Dumond (New York: D. Appleton-Century, 1934), 1:414.
[7] A. E. Grimké to T. Weld and John G. Whittier, August 20, 1837, *ibid.,* 1:427.
[8] T. Weld to S. and A. Grimké, October 10, 1837, *ibid.,* 1:453.

with her fiancé shows her to have been very anxious to meet her new
responsibilities and to dispel her reputation as an unnatural woman:

> *Beloved, I* believe *thou wilt find me* most *happy in our
> little cottage and in the kitchen of that cottage when duty
> calls me there;*. . . *May the Lord Jesus help me for thy sake,
> and for* woman's *sake to prove that well regulated minds
> can with* equal ease *occupy high and low stations and find*
> true happiness in both.[9]

Despite repeated pleas that they take up their old work once again, both
Sarah and Angelina remained almost completely taken up with the
problems of running a household, raising children, coping with female
health crises, and running a school to make ends meet.

WOMAN AND SLAVE

The vision of a more total human liberation, which Frances Wright
spoke of and which the Grimkés seemed to sense in the combined causes
of woman and slave, was not realized by the abolition movement. And
at the time it was unlikely that such an association could have been
maintained, for many of those who were able to make common cause
on antislavery were quite traditionalist on every other social issue, and
especially so on women.

   It becomes difficult to determine at times whether the consciousness
of woman's rights emerged mainly because of the antislavery movement
or in spite of it. It is true that women developed both politically and
socially through their involvement in the movement, yet it is also true
that while their labors were accepted, these women were not really
given due recognition by their brothers. It is often thought that the
very rebuffs that abolitionist women experienced were responsible for
the awareness of women's oppression that eventually led to the Seneca
Falls convention of 1848. Yet, viewed in the broader historical context,
the fact that the woman question arose at all within the abolition movement becomes evidence of the generally growing consciousness of
woman's changing roles: in the factory and the schoolhouse or semi-
nary, women were responding to the changes and preparing for the future.

[9] A. E. Grimké to T. Weld, April 29, 1838, *ibid.*, 2:649.

Gentility and Feminism

The woman movement had a base among the most domesticated wives in the land. The rapid changes that the family as an institution was undergoing, however, unavoidably affected the attitudes of all women.

The clearest organizational manifestation of the revolt of genteel women was the temperance movement. As early as the 1840s temperance was an infinitely more respectable cause than abolitionism or woman's rights. Not until the last quarter of the century did the temperance cause become a movement, but as a crusade it served as an early focus for the discontents, anger, and fears that middle-class women felt in their position within the institutions of marriage and family.

The quiet revolt of middle-class women was submerged and isolated from women's organized revolt and buffered from the sobering realities that women confronted in factories. These middle-class women were full-time housewives; they had not yet become the parasitic ladies of leisure, reading novels and engaging in ostentatious but trivial pursuit to pass the tiresome hours. Ladies of leisure would constitute a class only late in the century. For now, the middle class felt the need to erect its moral code as a bulwark against the classes above and below.

DOMESTIC NOVELS: THE UNDERGROUND REVOLT

The underground revolt of middle-class American women found expression in the best-selling domestic novels of the day. Sentimentalized and romanticized, the life of the middle-class woman was presented in all its detail in these books. Glory, heroism, and drama were discovered in the daily round of the housewife's chores, trials, and joys. However, there was rebellion beneath the surface:

> *No man, fortunately for his peace of mind, ever discovered that the domestic novels were handbooks of another kind of feminine revolt—that these pretty tales reflected and encouraged a pattern of feminine behavior so quietly ruthless, so subtly vicious that by comparison the ladies of Seneca appear angels of innocence.*[10]

[10] Helen W. Papashvily, *All the Happy Endings* (New York: Harper, 1956), p. xvi. The "ladies of Seneca" above refers to the women at the historic Woman's Rights Convention held in Seneca Falls, New York, in 1848.

The novels in question were not flights into a world of fantasy for bored housewives, but realistic, if somewhat overdone, accounts of American women in their everyday lives. The novels were almost anti-male in their outrage, disgust, condescension, and pity with regard to the "stronger sex." Many of the novels read almost like marriage manuals, with direct advice to the feminine audience on how to cope with male infidelity, neglect, passions, etc. The social tenor of the period was such that women novelists could reach a mass female audience only with *domestic* novels, even though these women novelists in their own lives offered examples of far more independent, experienced, and self-supporting women.

SEX AND THE MORAL CODE

Coursing under society's general preoccupation with virginity, chastity, seductions, and ravishings is the deep frustration caused by a moral code, strongest among the middle class, that at once both denied women the existence of sensual pleasures and regarded them as such sexual beings as to offer constant temptation to any male.

The intense public concern for the virginity and chastity of the middle-class woman seems to have been a general trait for the Victorian period, in Europe and in America. There were many crusades during the period, but the debate on the sexual life of the genteel woman seems to have been an all-pervasive one. The intent seems to have been to ban any sexual experience for women that was not directly connected with conjugal duties and procreation. Correspondingly, there were campaigns against masturbation and all things that might lead to this sin in both sexes. The existence of this "solitary vice" among girls was variously attributed to tight corseting and lascivious reading matter—especially domestic novels.

Accompanying the obsession with feminine morality was an almost morbid fascination with the ailments of the female body. Mrs. Lydia E. Pinkham founded a lifetime business on the "delicacy" of the female constitution:

> *Lydia E. Pinkham's Vegetable Compound . . . for prolapsus uteri or falling of the Womb and other female weaknesses*

including leucorrhoea, irregular and painful menstruation,
inflammation and ulceration of the womb . . . .[11]

CATHARINE BEECHER

The concerned but nonfeminist middle-class matron of the nineteenth century had public models in the many educated women lecturers and writers of the period. Foremost among them perhaps was Catharine E. Beecher. Catharine E. Beecher sought to elevate the duties of the house-wife to a science and also championed women's education. As we have noted, she believed education should better prepare women for their responsibilities in the home and, if the need should arise, in the labor market.

Although she was of necessity self-supporting and fully independent, Catharine Beecher stood apart from the woman movement. An out-spoken opponent of the movement, her concept of the condition of women and the evils of the woman movement stands as the epitome of the attitudes of what might be called the progressive genteel woman:

> *We agree . . . that woman's happiness and usefulness are*
> *equal in value to those of man's, and, consequently, that*
> *she has a right to equal advantages for securing them. We*
> *agree, also, that woman, even in our own age and country,*
> *has never been allowed such equal advantages, and that*
> *multiplied wrongs and suffering have resulted from this*
> *injustice.*
>
> *Finally, we agree that it is the right and the duty of every*
> *woman to employ the power of organization and agitation,*
> *in order to gain those advantages which are given to the*
> *one sex, and unjustly withheld from the other . . . .*

But, she continues:

> *This woman movement is one which is uniting by cooperat-*
> *ing influences, all the antagonisms that are warring on the*
> *family state. Spiritualism, free-love, free-divorce, the vicious*
> *indulgences consequent on unregulated civilization, the*
> *worldliness which tempts men and women to avoid* large

[11] Gerald H. Carson, *One for a Man, Two for a Horse* (Garden City, N.Y.: Double-day, 1961), p. 18.

families, often by sinful methods, thus making the ignorant masses the chief supply of the future ruling majorities.[12]

This statement, written in 1872, represents the increased anxiety over the stability of the family that characterized the period after the Civil War; nevertheless, the views that Miss Beecher espoused were essentially the same ones that feminists had been confronted with from the rank-and-file women of their class in the 1850s and 1860s as the woman movement began to take more vigorous form.

Regardless of Catharine Beecher's political views, she acknowledged that women did have real grievances and, even, that they had the right to *organize* and *agitate* to improve their condition. Thus, her statement gives evidence of a basic sympathy in consciousness between the genteel and the feminist woman. However, Catharine Beecher's criticisms of the woman movement also give us a direct line to the popular attacks made on feminism and, further, expose precisely those points on which most feminists were extremely defensive and vulnerable. In effect, her criticisms reveal the middle-class content of the woman movement.

FEMINISM AND THE FAMILY

The feminist counterparts to genteel womanhood shared a concern for woman's central position in the family. The woman movement saw the married woman as the victim of a whole range of restrictions that prevented her from realizing her individual potentialities *as* she met her primary duties of domesticity and gentility. In its early period, the movement concentrated more on the legal and social rights of women than on suffrage. There were drives to win for women the rights to own and control their own property, to divorce their husbands, and to retain guardianship of their children after the death, divorce, or desertion of the father; there were demands to stop the double standard in morals, and drives to release women from the disabling and disfiguring fashions then current. Conservative feminists argued for the vote eventually *because,* they reasoned, it would allow women to exercise their maternal and moral influence on the world outside the home while protecting that home as well.

[12] Catharine E. Beecher, *Woman's Profession as Mother and Educator, with Views in Opposition to Woman Suffrage* (Philadelphia: George Maclean, 1872), pp. 4, 5.

Spiritualism and free love were twin horrors that most feminists were as anxious as their more retiring sisters to exorcise from the movement. The life-styles and libertarian erotic ideas of Frances Wright and of the feminist sisters Victoria Woodhull and Tennessee Clafin met with violent reactions both within and without the woman movement, except among those few with a more catholic outlook, such as Elizabeth Cady Stanton and Susan B. Anthony.

Similarly the mainstream of the woman movement shunned the many utopian groups that went beyond discussions and proposals for legal reforms of the institutions of marriage and family. Along with health and food fads, marriage reform had been the pastime of many a radical intellectual. Collectivists and associationists debated the perfection of the marriage relationship. Collectivists could choose from a handful of communal societies if they wished to practice what they preached. The associationist view of marriage envisioned families living together with "combined kitchens" and "combined households" but *not* with "combined wives." Far from wishing to destroy the family, associationists would purify it of the drudgery, the disciplinary and custodial burdens, leaving only affection, confidence, and virtue.[13] These collectivists and associationists, among them the New England transcendentalists, and other free-spirited emancipationists who flourished in the 1840s and 1850s did not, however, survive into the post–Civil War period.

On the question of divorce, while a reform of divorce procedures in favor of women was urged by a number of feminists prior to the Civil War, none would have wanted free divorce. Furthermore, the difference between Catharine Beecher's position on divorce (that it was one of the antagonisms warring on the family state) and the feminist one was more strategic than anything else. Neither Miss Beecher nor the feminists wished to bring down the family; the feminist purpose in advocating divorce reform was to use the possibility of divorce as a protection for wife and children from a cruel, drunken, or vagrant husband and father.

Miss Beecher's contention that the woman movement led to the temptation "to avoid *large* families," while it may have been an almost obligatory argument in public lectures on the subject of genteel womanhood, had ceased to arouse as much sympathy among the mass of American women. As the nineteenth century wore on, women came

[13] Sidney Ditzion, *Marriage Morals and Sex in America. A History of Ideas* (New York: Bookman Associates, 1953), pp. 144–147.

increasingly to believe that it made more sense to raise a few children in good health than to bear ten or more for the grave. This change in attitude toward prolific maternity was also reflected in the popular literature of the day—women's magazines and domestic novels. Children were becoming less an economic asset and more an economic liability among the middle class.

GENTEEL WOMANHOOD VS. FEMINISM: ELIZABETH CADY STANTON

Feminists were those middle-class women who for a variety of reasons found it necessary and advantageous to go outside the home, possibly becoming self-supporting, in order to solve the problems in woman's condition that genteel women still believed could be righted from within the family. As one social historian expresses it: "Feminism was the reverse side of gentility, affecting women of the same social class who, as a result of industrialization, had become 'disemployed' in family production."[14] It would not be until around 1900 that the values and approaches of genteel and feminist women would have altered enough to allow a mass movement of middle-class women.

This difference in attitude of genteel and feminist women is brought sharply into focus by the writings and life of Elizabeth Cady Stanton. Author of the 1848 Declaration of Sentiments presented to the Seneca Falls women's convention, she was also a wife and the mother of a large and active family, and could thus speak from firsthand knowledge the unvarnished truth on women's lives:

> The general discontent I felt with woman's portion as wife, mother, housekeeper, physician, and spiritual guide, the chaotic conditions into which everything fell without her constant supervision, and the wearied, anxious look of the majority of women impressed me with a strong feeling that some active measures should be taken to remedy the wrongs of society in general, and of women in particular.[15]

[14] Fred Vigman, *Beauty's Triumph* (Boston: Christopher, 1966), p. 57.
[15] Elizabeth Cady Stanton, *Eighty Years and More* (1898, reprint ed., New York: Schocken Books, 1971), pp.147–148.

Elizabeth Cady Stanton was impatient of attempts that sought to improve women's status and condition by manipulating men. Within the family the incessant chipping away at male dominance by outwardly meek housewives was based on moralistic and emotional appeals to bind the men to the home. The Stanton approach was at once more realistic and more revolutionary:

> Let us condemn the system which makes men and women what they are and not crucify the victims of our false standard of morals. . . . Instead of hounding men, emancipate women from all forms of bondage. But so long as women are slaves, men will be knaves.[16]

But then, Mrs. Stanton said and wrote what many women knew and felt but did not dare to admit even to themselves. From her diary in 1883:

> Walt Whitman seems to understand everything in nature but woman. In "There is a Woman Waiting for Me," he speaks as if the female must be forced to the creative act, apparently ignorant of the great natural fact that a healthy woman has as much passion as a man, that she needs nothing stronger than the law of attraction to draw her to the male.[17]

Elizabeth Cady Stanton's views were, perhaps, atypical. She maintained her eloquent support for marriage reform and church reform long after her sisters in the movement had moved on to the less controversial political rights.

She did, however, share with many leaders of the early woman movement a personal familiarity with the life of a middle-class matron. Indeed, many early feminists were married and raised large families. (Single women, such as Susan B. Anthony, were no strangers to domestic cares either; she and many others had raised their own orphaned sisters and brothers, or nieces and nephews. Single women also spent

[16] Harriot Stanton Blatch and Theodore Stanton, eds., *Elizabeth Cady Stanton,* as quoted in Aileen S. Kraditor, *The Ideas of the Woman Suffrage Movement 1890–1920* (New York: Columbia University Press, 1965), p. 114.

[17] Blatch and Stanton, *Elizabeth Cady Stanton,* as quoted in Milton Rugoff, *Prudery and Passion: Sexuality in Victorian America* (New York: G. P. Putnam's Sons, 1971), p. 181.

long hours as nurses or baby-sitters for the children of their married friends in the movement.)

The Civil War and Its Aftermath

From 1848 until the Civil War, members of the woman movement were busy conducting annual conventions, pioneering petition campaigns, and gathering their forces. The work centered in New York State, under the energetic and inspirational guidance of Elizabeth Cady Stanton and Susan B. Anthony. When the crisis over slave labor erupted in the Civil War, there was mounting pressure on the woman movement to cease agitation. This particular juncture in history was said to be the "Negro's hour," while "woman's hour" was yet to come.

The black feminist Sojourner Truth, who organized and lectured in the North, spoke up during this period against neglecting the rights of black *women* in the rush to win rights for the black *man*:

> There is a great stir about colored men getting their rights, but not a word about the colored women; and if colored men get their rights, and not colored women theirs, you see the colored men will be masters over the women, and it will be just as bad as it was before. So I am for keeping the thing going while things are stirring; because if we wait till it is still, it will take a great while to get it going again.[18]

However, from 1861 until after the war, all activity specifically feminist in nature stopped. Under the leadership of Miss Anthony and Mrs. Stanton, the National Woman's Loyal League was organized, which, among other things, mounted a successful petition campaign of support for the Thirteenth Amendment to the Constitution.

The Civil War, as every war with general mobilization before and since, brought special pressures to bear on women's social and economic roles and the respective ideologies supporting these roles. The postwar years saw a fading of interest in communal societies such as the Oneida community in upstate New York and, within the woman movement, a similar lessening of interest in issues such as divorce and double standards of morality. The movement became a more sober and pragmatic one,

[18]Quoted in Mary R. Beard, *America Through Women's Eyes* (New York: Macmillan, 1933), pp. 231–232.

geared ever more to win for women a constitutional amendment, as the slaves had just done.

The postwar era offered the genteel woman a wider scope of expression. Women's clubs and petition campaigns became more respectable activities, and women were no longer restricted to the more indirect, insidious methods of influencing the male sex to reform itself and society. This change in climate was reflected in the waning influence of *Godey's Lady Book.* This magazine had enjoyed long years of wide circulation under the impressive editorship of Sarah Josepha Hale. Under the cloak of impeccable genteel respectability, Mrs. Hale had been in the habit of slipping in carefully couched criticisms of the position of women in society. In her pages there appeared on occasion articles on child development, feminine health and hygiene, and female education. After the Civil War, however, women wanted more than these veiled hints as to future steps.

Conclusion

Most participants in the woman movement differed with their class's view on the position of women but were profoundly middle class in every other way. Most importantly, as members of a class with predominantly business interests, they distrusted the giant corporate monopolies as well as the laboring classes, fearing control by the one and inundation by the other. They feared the collective nature of both.[19]

As the movement entered its final phase, many feminists would come to resemble professional social workers, with their concern for women's everyday problems restricted to the plight of immigrant, working-class, or poor women—the outcast and wretched. Pity and moral condemnation were mingled in the feminists' view of the lack of decorous and genteel relations between the sexes, for one example, in the lower class. In an era when childbirth was still a risky proposition, these feminists might have rebelled against the notion set forth by Catharine Beecher in her critique of the woman movement that they and their middle-class sisters should, in effect, lay down their lives in childbearing to ensure a well-populated middle class for future generations, but they did share Miss Beecher's fear of the working and poor classes.

[19] *Ibid.,* pp. 258–259.

Pity, moral condemnation, and fear were also at work in the attitude of these white, middle-class feminists toward black women leaders in the late nineteenth century. Furthermore, the drive for broader support of woman suffrage emphasized the need to win the backing of the white-supremacist South. By the 1880s the woman movement had become militantly bourgeois, joining in the general stream of antiblack, antilabor, and anti-immigrant philosophy that ran so high during the period. And while this trend was softened by the Reform Era, in the early twentieth century, with the settlement house movement and a general awareness, even among the women's clubs, of the plight of the working class and of immigrants in urban centers, the self-consciously bourgeois nature of the mainstream of the movement held until the passage of the suffrage amendment.

chapter 6

From the Civil War to 1920

Suffrage and Reform

From the Civil War up until the close of the nineteenth century, supporters of the woman movement continued their dedicated round of petition campaigns and lecture tours. There were a few women who refused to pay taxes, as there had been in isolated cases earlier, and in the 1870s a number of women tried to vote.

The same changes in women's economic and social spheres that brought into existence the woman movement also brought about changes in women's legal status, and at long last reforms were made in the area of property rights, divorce procurement, and guardianship of children. The suffrage movement was turning out many leaders and developing factions reflecting current trends on the social and political scene.

In January 1868, Elizabeth Cady Stanton and Susan B. Anthony founded the militant journal *The Revolution,* bearing the motto, "Men their rights and nothing more! Women their rights and nothing less!" This journal was to serve as the organ for the National Woman Suffrage Association, started in 1869 by radical New York suffragists. This group had a broad concept of woman's rights. Both Mrs. Stanton, with her background in abolitionist work and extensive interests, and Susan B. Anthony, with her experience in both abolition and temperance societies and working women's protective associations, saw the vote as a step toward greater social reforms for women. For *tactical* reasons, Susan B. Anthony concentrated on woman suffrage to the exclusion of any other efforts.

Their opposite numbers formed the American Woman Suffrage Association later in 1869, with its journal the *Woman's Journal*. This group represented what was to become the mainstream of the suffrage movement right up to its culmination in the attainment of the vote in 1920. It comprised women from the professional class and from backgrounds of moderate or independent wealth who considered the vote to be virtually the only right they lacked.[1]

Regional Development of the Woman Movement

It is deceptive to look at the course that the woman movement took in two regions such as the West and the South toward the end of the nineteenth century and to attribute the differences simply to the progressive nature of the one and the sluggish, feudalistic nature of the other. It is said that the preponderance of males in the West both raised the prestige of women and made possible their greater liberation; of the South it is said that the vestiges of social coercion left over from the slave system continued to hold women in check in the post–Civil War period. Actually in the last few decades of the century, class and race interests combined in *both* regions to create a relatively more favorable climate, at least for woman suffrage, than had existed in those areas previously.

THE WEST

In most parts of the West, excepting Utah, the imbalance in the sex ratio was severe. Women had not been following men westward in sufficient numbers. Catharine Beecher, with her missionary's zeal, saw the wild West as unspoiled territory waiting for women "to recreate in the wilderness the highminded domesticity of the East."[2] Nevertheless, in 1869, Wyoming, for example, had less than 2,000 women to its 8,000 men. Among adults the ratio was even more imbalanced. In this situation woman suffrage came to be viewed as a tool to improve the region's image for prospective female settlers and as a stabilizing factor in political life.

[1] Aileen S. Kraditor, *The Ideas of the Woman Suffrage Movement 1890–1920* (New York: Columbia University Press, 1965), pp. 261–262.
[2] Barbara M. Cross, *The Educated Woman in America. Selected Writings of Catharine Beecher, Margaret Fuller, and M. Carey Thomas* (New York: Teachers College Press, Columbia University, 1965), p. 1.

Not incidentally, the established citizens of the West appreciated the fact that woman suffrage would just about double the vote of the respectable, home-owning family man. Thus, in 1869, the same year that the transcontinental railroad was completed, woman suffrage came to Wyoming.[3] These Western legislators were not so much convinced of the equality of the sexes when they granted woman suffrage as they were eager for the flourishing of the white, middle-class, educated vote. In that context the social and political value of females was bound to rise.

In Utah, which granted woman suffrage in 1870, the public relations rewards of such a measure were foremost in the minds of the legislators. Woman suffrage was viewed as a masterful way for Mormonism to refute those who attacked the polygamous marriage as a lecherous institution that enslaved women in its harems. Several years earlier, in Tennessee, Mary Boykin Chesnut had written: "There are no Negro sexual relations half so shocking as Mormonism; and yet the United States makes no bones of receiving Mormons into its sacred heart."[4] Actually, Congress would soon pass a law banning polygamy.

In most of the Western states and territories where woman suffrage was granted in the nineteenth century, the immediate consequences for the general populace were negligible. The effects upon the woman movement, however, were considerable. The handful of suffrage victories in the West encouraged several generations of suffragists to continue the dreary battles to win state constitutional amendments on the question.

THE SOUTH

The social controls on women in the South were such that *organized* activity on their part or on their behalf was stymied. There are stories to the effect that Southern feminine service during the Civil War amounted to nothing more than saying no to the young men who proposed marriage before going off to fight the Yankees. Actually, Southern women were involved in a variety of relief operations during the war and shared some of the same grievances as their sisters in the North and the West. Moreover,

---

[3] Alan P. Grimes, *The Puritan Ethic and Woman Suffrage* (New York: Oxford University Press, 1967), p. 52.
[4] *A Diary from Dixie*, ed. B. A. Williams (Boston: Houghton Mifflin, 1949), p. 200.

their nonparticipation during the abolition struggles did not prove their indifference to the principles and realities involved. It was said that all true Southern women were abolitionists and hated slavery more than Mrs. Stowe.[5]

The white middle-class constituency that the woman movement appealed to was more responsive in the South to the message and methods of the temperance movement than to the program of the suffrage movement. The W.C.T.U. offered Southern women a sedate forum from which to attack male behavior. Through their limited campaigns against liquor and venereal disease they struck out at the more conspicuous expressions of male dominance in daily life, and, at the same time, they contributed to their own social and political development as active women.[6] However, in a culture where most of the women were still bound quite closely to home and family, the leadership of such a movement could easily be quite divorced from the common woman. This was, of course, a problem that the woman movement faced nationally; it was only more pronounced in the South.

The inroads that the suffrage movement was able to make in the South during the 1890s were made possible by forces that had little to do with woman's equality. As it was recognized that female suffrage would indeed multiply the strength of the white, Protestant, native-born electorate, public sentiment on the issue underwent a shift. To be sure, antisuffragists in the South continued to offer arguments that the North had heard fifty and sixty years earlier. Nevertheless, a number of Southern women rose to prominent local and national positions in suffrage organizations. The anti-immigrant sentiments of the North and the anti-black sentiments of the South worked hand in glove to help swell suffrage ranks. By 1890 the ideological differences between the two camps in the national suffrage movement had been largely erased; Elizabeth Cady Stanton and Susan B. Anthony had both moved to the right in the general atmosphere of ethnic and racial prejudice that surrounded them. A merger of the two groups produced the National American Woman Suffrage Association in 1890.

[5] Mary R. Beard, *America Through Women's Eyes* (New York: Macmillan, 1933), p. 204.
[6] Anne Firor Scott, *The Southern Lady from Pedestal to Politics 1830–1930* (Chicago: University of Chicago Press, 1970), p. 144.

The Woman Movement and the Working Class

FEMINISTS AND THE LABOR MOVEMENT

Working women had been organizing in increasing numbers during the nineteenth century. However, it is not surprising in view of the ever-increasing polarization of classes that the working women's drive for rights in union and factory made little contact with the middle-class woman movement. By the turn of the century, while many suffragists and other feminists held views that were outright racist and anti-working class, others remained seemingly unaware that the "pseudo-democratic refusal to recognize class distinctions in discussions of the woman question" concealed a program anti-working class in content and orientation. Moreover, the woman movement almost consistently tailored its demands to the specific needs not of working-class but of middle-class women.[7]

Individual feminists had come out for equal pay for equal work and the improvement of working conditions for women in factories, but such support was usually mostly rhetorical. In 1837, Sarah Grimké stressed the effects of women's inferior status upon the "laboring classes," and in 1868 both Elizabeth Cady Stanton and Susan B. Anthony were delegates to the convention of the National Labor Union—the former from a suffrage organization and the latter from a working women's protective association. The National Labor Union, in lending some support to Mrs. Stanton, was careful to emphasize that it was endorsing only her interest in labor, *not* her views on woman's rights.[8] In those early days, woman suffrage was still too controversial an issue to be endorsed without trepidation by the labor movement.

Revolution, the woman's journal edited by Mrs. Stanton and Susan B. Anthony from 1868 to 1870, contained numerous articles on wage-earning women. The articles urged working women to organize and to cooperate with male unionists where this was to their advantage. However, in 1869 an incident between Miss Anthony and the New York printers' union caused further estrangement between the woman and labor movements. Susan B. Anthony had long been interested in helping more women become printers. In 1854 the National Typographical Union had resolved to bar women from becoming compositors, and

[7]Edith Abbott, *Women in Industry* (New York: D. Appleton, 1910), pp. 8–9.
[8]Mary R. Beard, *The American Labor Movement* (New York: Macmillan, 1931), p.76.

within this context Miss Anthony felt it necessary to go to the employers during a strike in 1869 with a proposal for training women to become printers. She felt she was justified in doing this in order to expand women's opportunities for industrial education. Needless to say, however, the union interpreted her action as a stab in the back and as further proof of the unreliability of women as comrade unionists and of the woman movement in general. It is likely that Miss Anthony's carefully worded statement, which appeared shortly thereafter in the *New York Sun*, did not entirely clear up the conflict:

> My advice to all the women compositors of the city is now, as it has ever been since last autumn, to join the women's union, for in union alone there is strength, in union alone there is protection. Everyone should scorn to allow herself to be made a tool to undermine the just prices of men workers; and to avoid this union is necessary. Hence I say, girls, stand by each other, and by the men, when they stand by you.[9]

The labor movement and the woman movement did not share much mutual trust.

A NEW COALITION

After the turn of the century maturing forces within the union movement and within the woman movement created a meeting ground for unionist and feminist. This new climate was in part due to the entrance of two new groups, relatively silent in previous decades, into the politics of national woman's rights organizations—working-class and upper-class women. Working women had managed to develop their own leaders gradually, largely without any aid or encouragement from established unions. These women labor leaders were then able to attend suffrage conventions and speak eloquently in their own behalf.[10]

The activism of women who in the previous generation would have been among Mrs. Astor's four hundred select men and women of New York high society was perhaps part of a tide of disapproval of waste and decadence. The lady of leisure had become the target of much

[9] Alice Henry, *The Trade Union Woman* (New York: D. Appleton, 1915), p. 250.
[10] Kraditor, *Woman Suffrage Movement*.

criticism. Charlotte Perkins Gilman, the radical feminist ideologue, called her the "Priestess of the Temple of Consumption" and warned that the vicarious social and economic position of women was ruining the race, corrupting the economy, and producing a home atmosphere that crippled children both mentally and physically. Thorsten Veblen, who made the status of women the subject of much of his writing, predicted from his studies of the leisure class, that the natural human instinct for workmanship would lead women to throw off their useless and dependent existence as ornaments to the entrepreneurial class and return to a more socially productive role.

Some of these upper-class women were participants in the founding of the new organization that provided the framework for unionist and feminist cooperation. When the Women's Trade Union League was formed in 1903, women of wealth made up the majority of the organization's leadership, and continued to do so until 1907. Thereafter it and other organizations provided an arena where heiresses and factory operatives could be found working together.

The finest hour of the W.T.U.L. came in 1909 in New York City during the historic shirtwaist makers' strike. W.T.U.L. members helped raise strike funds, served on the picket lines, were arrested, and, of course, provided publicity and contacts for powerful reform-minded people in New York City. Such was the popular appeal of the shirtwaist makers' strike that the suffrage movement also gave material and propaganda assistance to the striking women. The National American Woman Suffrage Association lent its active support and that of its *Woman's Journal.*

As far as the majority within the woman movement was concerned, therefore, there had been successful recruitment of women from all classes by the second decade of this century. Suffragists could point to the 1903 report of the National American Woman Suffrage Association's Committee on Industrial Problems Affecting Women and Children, which presented the new recruiting policy. The Committee proposed that the strategic objectives be to recruit from both the working class and the leisure class, appealing to the "Divine Motherhood" that supposedly united women of all classes.[11]

[11] Clara B. Colby, *NAWSA Proceedings,* as quoted in Kraditor, *Woman Suffrage Movement, p. 152.*

However, individuals within and outside of the movement continued to brand the blurring of class issues—specifically the neglect of the specific needs of working-class women—as a deep failing of the suffragists and of the entire woman movement. It was well and good for wealthy and well-educated women to make a "profession" of the suffrage cause or the plights of the working woman, but, as Jessie Ashley pointed out in *Woman's Journal*, "Great wrongs are not suffered by handsome ladies as a class, but they are suffered by the working class as a whole.[12]

Jessie Ashley and others charged that the preponderance of well-to-do women in the leadership, at the conventions, on the committees, in the delegations to congressional hearings, and in all the work "through channels" had the effect of alienating the movement from poor and working-class women. Even those working-class women in the movement were becoming estranged from their working-class sisters. In her most damning accusation of class bias within the woman movement, particularly on the part of the suffragists, Jessie Ashley asked:

> *Had they ever come forward with vigorous support for purely working-class legislation? Had they ever shown themselves ready to back laws that would help workers but at the same time wipe out their own dividends?*[13]

During the decade from 1910 to 1920 there were many other individuals of differing political persuasions who were concentrating on women's problems and who saw them as linked to the class divisions within society. Most active in this regard were the socialists and anarchists.

Socialists, Anarchists, and the Woman Movement

THE SOCIALIST PARTY

The Socialist Party, founded in 1901, inherited the analysis of the condition of women as developed by Karl Marx, Friedrich Engels, and August Bebel. In this analysis, the subjugation of woman by man was viewed as rooted in class oppression. The liberation of women was one of the accomplishments that were promised after the completion of a

[12] *Woman's Journal,* June 24, 1911, as quoted in *ibid.,* p. 158.
[13] *Woman's Journal,* April 22, 1911, as quoted in *ibid.,* p. 156.

socialist revolution, just as the liberation of men from alienating labor would also have to wait. While leading theoreticians often expressed considerable criticism of the oppression and exploitation of women, the analysis of the condition of women in capitalist society remained on a rather simplistic level.

Individual socialists, both men and women, exhibited all the contradictions and inconsistencies on the woman question that existed in the woman movement itself. Many socialists were in their private lives as Victorian as their unregenerate contemporaries when it came to granting women a real place in political and social spheres outside the home. For some women, the socialist movement was a community within which they were able to cast off many conventional strictures on their personal as well as political lives. However, for the most part, women in the socialist movement did nothing more revolutionary than serve as loyal supporters to their men at home and in the women's auxiliaries.

The relationship of Eugene Debs to the suffrage movement is an example of the ambivalence of most socialists toward the woman movement. During a meeting with Susan B. Anthony in 1903, Debs, always a public supporter of woman's rights, engaged in some banter: " 'Give us suffrage,' Miss Anthony said laughingly, 'and we'll give you socialism.' To which Debs blithely replied: 'Give us socialism and we'll give you suffrage.' "[14] Actually, Debs gave strong support to the passage of the Suffrage Amendment and was bitterly disappointed when the votes he received in the first post–woman suffrage presidential election, in 1920, showed no real gain over his total in 1916.

His wife Katherine was to speak poignantly of the failure of the socialist movement to affect her own life. Katherine M. Debs was a political person; although not very active in the socialist movement, she did write an article supporting woman suffrage, "The Right of Women to Vote," published in 1910. Yet, her personal life did not seem enriched by her association with the movement. Her husband's comrades did not become her own, and she had no fulfilling circle of her own:

> *For him the labor movement had become thousands of brothers; for her it remained a faceless mass. . . . Owning few friends, recoiling from women's clubs and civic*

[14] Ray Ginger, *The Bending Cross. A Biography of Eugene Victor Debs* (New Brunswick: Rutgers University Press, 1949), p. 224.

> *activities, she lived in self-imposed isolation from the warmth of social life. Day after day she remained in her ugly house-keeping rooms, reading novels, meticulously cleaning the furniture, resenting her condition.* [15]

Late in their marriage, during one of Debs's prison terms, Katherine Debs could calmly say, in trying to ward off public attention: "the wives of great men always suffer by comparison, and people expect them to be as great as their husbands, when they know, that as a rule, great men marry inferior women." [16]

For a select minority of women the socialist movement provided an atmosphere in which they could thrive and make unique and creative contributions; however, the experience of Katherine Debs was perhaps typical of the failure of the movement to reach and transform the lives of most women.

EMMA GOLDMAN AND MARGARET SANGER

Two women originally in the socialist camp who overcame the familiar boundaries to women's experience and influenced many other women were Emma Goldman and Margaret Sanger. Both Emma Goldman and Margaret Sanger had a consciousness of women's condition that went beyond the traditional Marxist linking of women's history with class oppression. Both rebelled against the hypocrisy that allowed so many socialists to voice rhetorical support for women's rights while privately following a course of inaction or denial concerning women's needs. [17]

In background the two women were quite different. Emma Goldman came to this country as an immigrant with her family in the late nineteenth century. She came up through the ranks of factory unions, participating in several strikes before becoming a full-time anarchist jounalist and agitator. Born almost a generation later, Margaret Sanger came from a libertarian middle-class family in upstate New York. Mrs. Sanger learned of the conditions of working-class families through her work as a registered nurse in the slums of New York and as a result was later

[15] *Ibid.,* p. 61.
[16] *Ibid.,* p. 411.
[17] For a sensitive analysis of women and the Socialist Party during this period, see Mari Jo Buhle, "Women and the Socialist Party, 1901–1914," in *From Feminism to Liberation,* ed. Edith Hoshino Altbach (Cambridge, Mass.: Schenkman, 1971), pp. 65–86.

receptive to the ideas discussed among the socialist circles in which she and her husband William moved.

Both women edited and published radical journals oriented toward women's issues among others. Emma Goldman's journal *Mother Earth* (1906-1917) was doubtless an influence upon Margaret Sanger's journal *Woman Rebel*, which ran for seven issues after its founding in the spring of 1914. The very first issue of *Woman Rebel* contained an excerpt from Emma Goldman's essay "Love and Marriage" demanding the right of women not to be reduced to machines of reproduction.[18] Though Margaret Sanger lacked Emma Goldman's practical experience as an anarchist agitator in Chicago, she ardently championed her causes in print in her monthly magazine. Advocating political anarchism and taking a militant stance on the issue of women's liberation, she gained readers for *Woman Rebel* as far away as Europe, among them such prominent women as Ellen Key, Rosa Luxemburg, and the Pankhursts.

After Margaret Sanger's indictment under the Comstock Law (federal anti-obscenity legislation) for sending birth control information (*Woman Rebel*) through the mails, Emma Goldman was one of the first to collect funds for her and to embark on an extended public speaking tour in support of Margaret Sanger and the birth control issue.[19]

In supporting Margaret Sanger, Emma Goldman was also criticizing the established American woman movement for its "puritanical" shallowness in refusing to recognize the sexual rights of women and for its continued support of the ideal of gentility, which narrowed its vision of what true human liberation might be like. Taking issue with leaders of the woman movement such as Charlotte Perkins Gilman and Jane Addam Emma Goldman denounced their belief

> that all that was needed was independence from external tyrannies; the internal tyrants, far more harmful to life and growth—ethical and social conventions—were left to take care of themselves; and they have taken care of themselves.[20]

Throughout the nineteenth century there were many feminists who advocated celibacy as a practical alternative to the burdens and obstacles

---

[18] Richard Drinnon, *Rebel in Paradise. A Biography of Emma Goldman* (Boston: Beacon Press, 1970), p. 169.
[19] *Ibid.*, p. 152.
[20] *Ibid.*, p. 153.

that woman's traditional sexual roles inflicted. However, by the end of the century what had begun as a necessity had become transformed into a virtue, and it was the idea of the "compulsory vestal" embodied in most middle-class feminists against which Emma Goldman, Margaret Sanger, Ellen Key, and others were rebelling in the United States and abroad.[21]

Margaret Sanger referred to the "puritanical objections" she encountered from suffragists and feminists—"the up and doing progressive women":

> Most of them were shocked at the mention of abortion, while others were scarcely able to keep from laughing at the idea of my making a public campaign around the idea of too many children. "It can't be done," they said. "You are too sympathetic. You can't do a thing about it until we get the vote. Go home to your children and let things alone."[22]

Mrs. Sanger also leveled a very telling criticism at those social workers who, in Chicago, made it difficult for her to bring birth control information and services to the poor women of the stockyard district. (She was later to work successfully with social workers in the years after her early radical period.) The stockyard district had been well organized by social workers connected with the settlement Hull House; without their sanction contact with the local women was impossible. The social workers were not interested in birth control.

The reaction of some socialists to Margaret Sanger's work on sex education and birth control mirrored the age-old antifeminist adages of the whole nineteenth century. One critic even charged that Margaret Sanger would "produce a panic which would cause women to lose all confidence in men and cause them to withdraw their capital [themselves] from the marriage market."[23]

Further alienating Margaret Sanger from the socialist movement was the fact that the industrial strikes called for by the Industrial Workers of the World and others took the greatest toll from the women and children. There was no program to meet the special oppression and

[21] *Ibid.*, p. 153.
[22] Margaret Sanger, *An Autobiography* (New York: Norton, 1938), p. 131.
[23] Buhle, "Women and the Socialist Party," p. 85.

urgent needs of women with children, although the I.W.W. was of considerable moral and material help in those pre-war years.[24] Thus, Margaret Sanger perceived herself as cut off from the major radical and reform organizations and trends of the day—all of which drew back from birth control as a major issue, for strategic, ideological, or moral reasons.

Emma Goldman and Margaret Sanger parted ways increasingly after 1916. It was in that year that Margaret Sanger came to the realization that the working-class women upon whose support she had previously depended lacked the financial, social, and educational resources necessary to develop a worldwide birth control movement. What suffrage was for many feminists, birth control became for Margaret Sanger. However, just as she had criticized the reliance on the vote as a panacea, so Emma Goldman also rejected a reliance on birth control as the means of solving the economic and social ills of the world, especially when information and devices were to be controlled and disseminated by doctors, as Margaret Sanger insisted they be, and not by the people who needed them.

Unlike many other activist women during the period, Emma Goldman was hamstrung in her subsequent political work by continual harassment and persecution from the government. More accommodating and moderate in ideology and style, other formerly radical women were often able to graduate to a respectable status in the reform movements of the day. Margaret Sanger was unusual in her quick rise from the status of a public enemy (in the eyes of the law) to that of an honored and influential world figure. However, many of her contemporaries also moved swiftly from their agitational work and service among women in factories or among the "wives of the wage slaves" to positions in reform organizations such as the Women's Trade Union League or in government agencies such as the Labor Department's Women's Bureau (established under this name in 1920).

The New Woman in the Pre-War Era

While nearly all new impulses in women's lives were reflected somewhere in the broad spectrum of the woman movement, there was one type of woman with no representation. A new generation of middle-class young women had emerged, tied neither to the domestic sphere nor to the labor force. Brought to the cities in the wave of urban growth between

[24] Sanger, *Autobiography*, p. 79.

1890 and 1920, these women created a new female culture. The "flapper" may have been the woman of the 1920s, but the young women of the pre-World War I days were already making headlines with their dances, their new music, and their fashions. After the turn of the century, these women, who a generation earlier would have been genteel ladies, allowed themselves a sensualism, a glamor, and a frivolity that once passed for the indecency and vulgarity of the lower class. Magazines and newspapers proclaimed the "Day of the Girl" and "Sex O'Clock in America."[25]

During this period the woman movement was making its final push for suffrage and participating in several other social reform efforts; in the main, however, the energies of the movement had become focused on legislative reform, to the exclusion of all else. In the meantime, the movement lost all contact with the new type of city-bred young woman who no longer felt the need of the woman movement to chaperon her toward a life of greater liberation. This new female culture had very little, if any, feminist content. Sensing this, and reacting against the alien culture, some within the movement spoke out on the subject.

The established feminist and sometime Darwinist and socialist Charlotte Perkins Gilman had no sympathy for the new women and their culture. Her major criticism was directed against the new emphasis upon sex, deploring its socially regressive effect on women. In 1898 her book, *Women and Economics,* appeared, which attacked the "sexuo-economic" imbalance between the sexes:

> *Half the human race is forced to confine its productive human energies to the same channels as its reproductive sex-energies.*
>
> *The false economic position of women . . . sexualizes our industrial relation and commercializes our sex relation. And, in the external effect upon the market, the over-sexed woman, in her unintelligent and ceaseless demands, hinders and perverts the economic development of the world.*[26]

[25] James R. McGovern, "The American Woman's Pre-World War I Freedom in Manners and Morals," *Journal of American History* 55 (1968): 316.
[26] Charlotte Perkins Gilman, *Women and Economics. A Study of the Economic Relation as a Factor in Social Evolution,* ed. Carl N. Degler 1898. Reprint. (New York: Harper & Row, 1966), pp. 117, 120.

No doubt, part of her criticism was motivated by the personal revulsion Mrs. Gilman felt toward the new life-style. Nevertheless, she offered sound arguments when she interpreted women's more aggressive sexuality as one more means of stunting their total growth and as yet another way in which women would bind themselves to men.

Charlotte Perkins Gilman remained convinced that until the institutions of home and family were reformed to allow women to leave behind the custodial and routine parts of housework and child care, women would never become fully independent economically and, thus, liberated. She traced what she saw as woman's social, political, intellectual, even genetic, inferiority to a basic imbalance in the division of lifework between the sexes. Few, if any, feminists since Elizabeth Cady Stanton had been able to view women's rights and women's inferior status so broadly and profoundly. Not since Catharine Beecher had a woman subjected the roles of housewife and mother to such careful scrutiny. Needless to say, everything Charlotte Perkins Gilman advocated was a rejection of the kind of home economics preached by Catharine Beecher and her followers. Ironically, radical critiques of home and family did not appear relevant to the "frivolous" young women discussed above. After Charlotte Perkins Gilman, no one in the feminist tradition was left to carry on her unique perspectives on women.

Club Women

The women's club movement began in the nineteenth century, and its growth in a way paralleled that of other sectors of what has been broadly defined as the woman movement. Club women come last in this chapter because they were virtually the only organized group to survive intact the end of the suffrage movement. In fact, the women's club movement is unmatched in longevity by any other form of organized, specifically *women's* activity.

Including women's clubs in a discussion of the woman movement is not without its problems. During much of the history of the woman movement, feminists spoke with ridicule of ladylike club women whose respectability kept them from deep involvement in any of the issues of the day. Feminists on occasion also criticized the inability of club women to recognize their own subjugation as women.

However, women's clubs cannot so easily be dismissed from a history of women, as a comparative look at certain statistics will show. Until the last three decades of the suffrage movement, membership in suffrage organizations can hardly have amounted to more than 10,000 to 15,000 women. During this period, membership in the General Federation of Women's Clubs, drawn primarily from the middle class, rose quickly from 100,000 in 1896 to about 200,000 in 1900, to some 800,000 by 1910. During the decade from 1910 to 1920, the rise in the urban population and the general acceleration and coalescing of progressive forces resulted in a spurt of growth for all parts of the woman movement. As 1920 approached, the National American Woman Suffrage Association had some 2,000,000 members, and the militant Woman's Party, formed in 1917, swelled official suffrage ranks by 25,000 additional women. The development of the suffrage movement into a broad, moderate, and respectable social force cut into the lead in membership of the women's clubs, and the distinction between suffrage organization and women's club became blurred. In this last decade before the Suffrage Amendment, the General Federation of Women's Clubs finally passed a resolution endorsing equal suffrage for women. Prior to this time of rapid growth and joining of forces within the woman movement, however, the women's club was obviously the form of organization with which the majority of middle-class women were comfortable.

FROM CIVIL WAR TO WORLD WAR I

The women's club movement began in the 1860s, after the Civil War. Between 1890 and 1910, the new national women's organizations included the following: Daughters of the American Revolution, Colonial Dames of America, National Society of United States Daughters of 1812, United Daughters of the Confederacy, National Council of Jewish Women, National Association of Colored Women, National Federation of Afro-American Women, National Congress of Mothers, National Consumers' League, Women's Trade Union League, Young Women's Christian Association. By 1890 there were enough groups to form the General Federation of Women's Clubs.

Most of the women's clubs listed above were affiliated with the General Federation. Significantly absent, however, because they were barred from membership, were the black women's clubs. Black middle-class women had begun to organize nationally in the 1890s, as chronicled by the Boston journal *Woman's Era.*[27] A sampling of black women's organizations in Harlem after the turn of the century shows the variety of

[27] Eleanor Flexner, *Century of Struggle* (New York: Atheneum, 1970), p. 190.

interests: Utility Club, Utopia Neighborhood, Debutantes' League, Sempre Fidelis, Colored Branch of the YWCA, Alpha Kappa Alpha (a sorority of college women).[28] However, the attitude of the General Federation of Women's Clubs toward these black women's organizations shows that the leadership of the white women's club movement could relate to black women only as objects of charity.

Aside from the racism and class bias of the white women's clubs, there were also elements of female rebellion that entitle the women's club movement to be grouped within the broader woman movement. Sorosis, which is said to have been the first women's club, was formed by a group of women journalists after one of them was barred from a New York Press Club reception for Charles Dickens. Likewise, many of the other clubs were formed in reaction to the discrimination women encountered from men: the Daughters of the American Revolution was formed in 1890 to protest the policies of the Sons of the American Revolution. Although women's clubs appeared in many instances to be mere echoes of men's clubs, women's club leaders were anxious to establish the clubs on an independent footing, with their own specific purposes.

These purposes changed over the years. In the beginning all but strictly religious themes were prohibited for respectable ladies' groups, and until the mid-1890s, even philanthropic goals appeared to be highly controversial among club women. By the time women's clubs had become a national trend, a variety of cultural activities had become socially acceptable. However, in its earliest years, the General Federation of Women's Clubs reflected in its constitution the cautious and conservative nature of the clubs:

> *Article IV: Clubs applying for membership . . . must show that no sectarian or political test is required and that . . . their chief purpose is not philanthropic or technical, but social literary, artistic or scientific culture.*[29]

Between 1894 and 1896, the restrictions on philanthropic clubs were dropped by the General Federation. Many club women had sympathy

[28] Elise Johnson McDougald, "The Double Task. The Struggle of Negro Women for Sex and Race Emancipation," *The Survey* 53, no. 11 (March 1, 1925): 691.
[29] Sophonisba P. Breckinridge, *Women in the Twentieth Century* (New York: McGraw-Hill, 1933), pp. 17-18.

with the reform movements of the day and some maintained membership in other organizations. The 1898 resolutions of the General Federation's "Industrial Section" show how quickly the tone of the organization changed from literary to reformist: the resolutions asked for the establishment of postal savings banks for small wage earners; legislation against the labor of children under fourteen years of age; the availability of public education for all children up to age fourteen; the enactment of protective eight-hour labor laws for women and children; the standardization of labor legislation through the United States; the forming of committees in each club to investigate, pressure for, and work toward such reforms; and, finally, the appointment by the General Federation of a five-woman Committee on Legislation for Women and Children.[30]

In the last quarter of the century, one of the strongest organized supporters of woman suffrage was the Woman's Christian Temperance Union. During most of the 1880s and 1890s, under the leadership of Frances Willard, the W.C.T.U. espoused not only prohibition but also legal and social protection for women and children—in the home, in industry, in the professions, and in education. Because of the power of liquor interests upon state legislatures, the alliance with temperance was a mixed blessing for suffragists; temperance was caricatured in the public mind as the hysterical campaign of ax-wielding, hellfire-preaching Carry Nations. In fact, Carry Nation and the Anti-Saloon League were the black sheep of the temperance movement, a source of embarrassment to the genteel W.C.T.U. In any case, by the turn of the century, the W.C.T.U. had reverted to its single-issue orientation, discarding its association with the more radical reform causes of the day.

The height of the women's club movement spanned the years from the 1890s to World War I. It was during this period that the settlement house movement, the organizations of consumers, and the working-women's clubs (for women industrial workers) flourished. With the exception of the Women's Trade Union League, the orientation of women's clubs was markedly missionarylike and charitable. And one must admit that while club women may have been inspired by sincere compassion and devotion to their work, a strong element in their activities no doubt was a fascination in seeing "how the other half lives."[31]

[30] *Ibid.*, pp. 21–22.
[31] Flexner, *Century of Struggle*, p. 209.

THE CONSUMERS' LEAGUE AND THE WOMEN'S TRADE UNION LEAGUE

The difference between the Consumers' League and the Women's Trade Union League illustrates the range of consciousness and approach within the women's club movement. The W.T.U.L. was a women's club, but it was in the radical wing of the club movement. It straddled the line between the labor movement and the woman movement. The W.T.U.L.'s ability to establish a productive relationship with working women and the unions was unique not only among women's clubs but in the whole woman movement. The W.T.U.L. raised strike funds and provided emergency services to working women and helped spread an acceptance of unionism among women in industry.

The New York Consumers' League, formed in 1891, was in the conservative tradition of the reform period. It was not an exclusively female organization, although the membership and officers were predominantly women. Members of the League possessed a boundless faith in the prospects for America to extend to all its citizens and, in fact, to the whole world the fruits of its natural resources, technological progress, and democratic spirit.

One blighted area in this vista of progress was becoming unpleasantly conspicuous—the social relations and conditions produced by "the industrial advance." But the attitude of the Consumers' League toward labor was, it must be admitted, a unionist's nightmare:

> We never sentimentally put the rights of the employee above the rights of the employer. . . . We tried to adjust fairly the differences between employer and employee, through the power of the third factor, the consumer.[32]

"Uncle Sam's wife" was what members considered the League to be.

Nevertheless, the League in its investigations did unearth facts of exploitation of labor by employers. For example, the League discovered that in sixteen firms surveyed during the 1895 Christmas season, store clerks put in a total of over 600,000 hours of unpaid overtime. "This was the Christmas present made by the employees to their employers."[33]

---

[32] Maud Nathan, *The Story of an Epoch-Making Movement* (New York: Doubleday, Page, 1926), pp. 58–59.
[33] *Ibid.*, p. 35.

To alleviate the suffering of the store clerks, the League undertook a major campaign to educate the buying public to do their Christmas shopping earlier. This almost ludicrous response of the League shows the trust it placed in the power of the consumer and the League's tacit assumption that the store clerks could not themselves rectify the situation by banding together to demand fair standards of wages and hours.

Its condescending attitude toward labor notwithstanding, merchants were very hostile toward the activities of the League. Accustomed to a free rein over their predominantly young, female sales and clerical personnel—in the absence or inactivity of unions—merchants attacked the League as a group of "sentimental visionary women." Employers hit upon a particularly sensitive point when they asked the reform-minded matrons how they would feel if investigators invaded their own households to inquire as to the wages, hours, benefits, and working and living conditions of their domestic servants. The distinguished Dr. Mary Putnam Jacobi responded in a very revealing way:

> The function of the industrial business is the creation of wealth, the function of the household is the fulfilment of personal satisfactions, the creation, if possible, of happiness. . . . Hence, as a substitute for wealth, the special rewards of personal service are personal affection, appreciation of fidelity, trust, social honour.[34]

The same arguments used by Dr. Jacobi to justify the absence of standards in domestic service were used by paternalistic businesses to explain why their workers did not need a union. In fact, domestic servants were among the most exploited segments of the labor force. At that time domestic service was the most common form of female employment other than farm work. The inability of Consumers' League members to recognize their own part in exploiting female labor was, of course, not unique. Many suffragists and other feminists must have depended upon an underpaid staff to run their households while they went out to do reform work.

Even more noticeable among League members than this insensitivity to the position of domestic servants was the absence of any demands on their own behalf as women. Suffragists at least felt personally aggrieved by the deprivation of a political right; temperance workers fought the

[34] *Ibid.*, p. 31.

domination of the drunken husband over his wife and family; but moderate club women, epitomized by the members of the Consumers' League, saw themselves as lacking in no rights. The only self-image they projected through their work was that of a national conscience; they were the watchful guardians of others' rights. Women active in settlement houses at least worked or lived in working-class neighborhoods and learned new values and attitudes through their close association with poor and immigrant workers, and others. Club women could go far in their work without ever confronting their own lives as women and as members of a certain social class. They were sustained in their zeal and dedication by the resistance they daily encountered from businessmen, industrialists, managers, and employers of all sorts, which strengthened their conviction that their club activity was crucial work.

THE WOMEN'S CLUB MOVEMENT AND REFORM

Official histories of the women's club movement link it in retrospect with every reform movement in the nineteenth century. Such histories by club women usually attribute the origins of the club movement to a vague "awakening" of women and to an urge on their part to better society by congregating together and combining their efforts. In a strange juxtaposition of reforms, one history claimed that the club movement had fought for abolition, a spirit of mercy toward dumb animals, and the recognition of the human rights of women and children.[35] The slave, the dumb animal, and the woman or child in poverty and dire circumstance were all objects for the pity of club women.

Yet, for all the philanthropy, the main benefactors of the women's clubs were club women themselves. Clubs gave them a purpose, a place and a time to be active with others outside the familiar circles of home and church. The women's club was referred to by the women themselves as their "postgraduate" education. For many, club work also took the place of the profession they never had.

It is an indisputable fact that club women formed the most conservative, even reactionary, wing of the woman movement. It is also true that in many respects their busy charity work and self-improvement and literary circles served only to skirt the issues that the rest of the movement was facing to some degree—issues that concerned the eco-

---

[35] Jennie C. Croly, *The History of the Woman's Club Movement in America* (New York: H. G. Allen, 1898), pp. 10–12.

nomic, social, and political disfranchisement of women in America. However, for many of the women who joined women's clubs by the thousands, the clubs represented a kind of personal rebellion against a useless existence and against male control. Moreover, for many of these women, the women's club was the only way they could function outside the home.

Conclusion

For all intents and purposes, the woman movement came to an end with the passage in 1920 of the woman suffrage amendment. Not only had the major goal of the movement been accomplished, but increased opportunities in education, employment, leisure, and social contacts made it possible for middle-class women to make it on their own. Most of the benefits of the long struggle for woman's rights have gone to professional women, as is shown by the type of predominantly women's organizations characteristic of the postsuffrage period: the American Association of University Women, American Federation of Teachers, National Education Association of Women, National Federation of Business and Professional Women's Clubs, etc.

The National American Woman Suffrage Association became the League of Women Voters. The League is an organization with a diffuse purpose consisting of an educational program of lectures and discussions plus activities in support of various liberal causes. The organization has avoided developing specifically women's issues.

The National Woman's Party, which had revived a weakening suffrage movement through its militant program of civil disobedience, did survive after the Suffrage Amendment. Since 1921 the party has concentrated on the passage of a federal equal rights amendment that would eliminate all discrimination against, and protective legislation for women. However, the party's concentration on the federal legislation limited its vision in the postsuffrage era. Moreover, it alienated women labor unionists by its attack upon protective legislation.

The woman movement arose out of the mingling of political, social, economic, and cultural changes in the nineteenth century. And although only a minority of all American women were actually involved in the meetings, demonstrations, clubs and associations, the woman movement in its multiple phases and factions did throw light on all the conflicts and changes that informed the lives of American women during those years.

Conclusion

In the end, however, no amount of good will can change the fact that the woman movement, which we have defined as ending with the Suffrage Amendment in 1920, was incomplete. Although tactically the women of the suffrage movement placed their faith in a simple constitutional amendment, symbolically female suffrage represented more than the vote to both friend and foe. The passionate response the issue drew from feminists proved that they saw in suffrage the realization of women's dignity, strength, and worth in society. However, the Susan B. Anthony amendment left many problems unresolved.

Most of the controversial issues with which the movement struggled have returned in modern garb. The rights and the status of women in industry and of women in the professions remain in jeopardy; the work and the worth of the housewife remain an ambiguity; research seems to uncover more questions than answers about female intelligence and emotions; yet definitions of feminine and masculine nature still weigh heavily on the respective sexes. The women's liberation movement that is emerging today will have to cover much old ground. Nevertheless, the failures and successes of the woman movement of the past should serve as an instructive precedent and legacy to the present movement.

part 4

THE NEW FEMINISM

chapter 7

CONTEMPORARY WOMEN'S LIBERATION
THE feminist revival and twentieth-century dissent

The Revival of Feminism

After a lapse of two generations, the United States is experiencing a revival of feminism. Women at various levels of society are perceiving that the woman's issue was not settled with the attainment of the woman suffrage amendment in 1920. A wealth of ideological and organizational traditions had been accumulated by the several waves of feminist activity during the nineteenth and early twentieth centuries. Yet, these traditions were not passed on to a new generation of feminists. The manner in which the woman movement ended in the triumphant drive for the vote had, perhaps, given the illusion that American women had achieved the ultimate right. For a time, then, it appeared as if society would have no need for feminism again, and certainly not in the same century.

During the intervening years from 1920 to the late 1960s, there were many changes in women's lives. However, individual endeavor almost totally supplanted the collective commentary and agitation of the feminist movement. Officially, then, women were ushered into the great American tradition of rugged individualism: in streamlined homes, at school and university, and on the job women were to give and to receive according to individual abilities and merit. For two generations there was public acceptance of the belief that women were progressing on their own in all walks of life. In the absence of a feminist social movement, changes for the better in women's lives could be attributed in a diffuse way to the American Way of Life; changes for the worse were allowed to be discounted uncritically.

Remnants of the feminist past did, however, survive the 1920 culmination of the suffrage movement. The Women's Trade Union League, now down to a few local chapters, kept its national status until the 1950s, and a smattering of other women's clubs remained as vestiges of all the presuffrage activity. Working women have continued within unions and associations, though without quite the drama of the great battles in female labor history. In the women's caucuses of trade unions and in their own professional organizations women have tried to protect the gains they have achieved on the job. Although the women's liberation movement has not arisen from these older organizations, it has revitalized them, and their progress is linked now to the revival of feminism.

The new women's movement,[1] with its roots in the new left, encompasses only part of the initiative for change among American women. It has not yet had time to grow into the broad social movement of nineteenth- and early-twentieth-century feminism.

Other lines of initiative among women exist independent of the women's movement. Chief among these are the activities of women of an implicitly feminist outlook who have struggled, often alone and over decades, in their work—in professions, trade unions, the arts, or voluntary service. Until recently we have lacked that social climate necessary for a full response to their experiences and grievances and a full application of their insights. Now, however, as the constituencies of women's liberation grow, the new women's movement may rejuvenate a collective spirit among these experienced women.

Constituencies of the Women's Movement

CAMPUS GROUPS

One sensitive issue in a movement is always the constituencies among which it finds its strength. At the outset, the women's liberation movement drew its supporters in the main from among radical students, the highly educated but underemployed, and professionals, as have other social movements of the recent past.

The common link among these groups was higher education, and to be highly educated in this society usually means to be middle class and

[1] The new feminist movement is commonly referred to today as the "women's movement."

white. This kind of constituency has characterized all campus-based movements of the last decade, with the exception that support from among university faculty and other professional groups is somewhat stronger in the women's movement than it has been in other radical movements. Moreover, most participants in the women's movement who do not fit this typical race and class description have already moved away from their original communities through education and life-style. Thus, the women's movement appears to be the most recent one to involve highly advantaged constituencies.

Nevertheless, the women's movement does have new constituencies. First, and most obviously, there is a newness simply in the rise of the female members of the student and intellectual groups formerly dominated by the males. For women who were typically and consistently excluded or undervalued in organizations, the experience of being valued and accepted in a movement as a *birthright*—as a consequence of simply *being* female—was an astounding change. In every campus-based movement from the early civil rights period through the peace, free-speech, student power, and late SDS anti-imperialist movements, women were in subordinate positions. For now, what is significant is that the women are a fresh and hitherto untapped segment of the old campus-based constituencies.

HOUSEWIVES

The sparseness of nonstudent support was always a source of embarrassment to the new left. The shift to an ideology in the new left that marked students as part of a new oppressed white-collar class did not really end the defensiveness and uneasiness over the lack of traditional working-class support. As has already been admitted, the women's movement in its initial phase followed several phases of the new left. Like the new left, the women's movement at the outset has had its center of gravity in the college and university campuses.

The women's movement has, however, begun to change accepted patterns of support built up in the new left. No development illustrates this as readily and convincingly as the arrival of the constituency of housewives in the women's liberation movement. It was, after all, the situation of housewives to which Betty Friedan addressed herself in *The Feminine Mystique.* Even if this constituency remains largely within the educated middle class and thus does not broaden the social base of the movement, it nonetheless is the most vital and potentially creative component.

Via several approaches—legal, political, economic, etc.—the movement is centering on the lives of women as wives and mothers. And if many social and political analysts have not comprehended the broader implications of this shift in constituency, that is perhaps another measure of the long denial of the stature and substance of the housewife's role in society.

Now, a small number of housewives are overcoming their accustomed isolation to become the new hidden constituency of the women's movement. Perhaps their tentative steps to alter their lives can be compared to trends among white-collar and industrial workers to alter their jobs. Both domestic and labor sectors have undergone many decades of mechanization of the work process. In each case the technological advances have not necessarily led to the most effective or creative use of machines or people. The automation of the assembly line and the streamlining of the modern home have not been designed to cater to the needs of the people doing the work.

The housewives in the women's movement are women who because of their life-style would not have been involved in the new left. Housewives do not have a part in the struggles for student power in universities; mothers of young children do not easily expose themselves or their dependents to the danger of police confrontations and tear gas; and, finally, in their very identification with home and family, housewives epitomize the strictures of middle-class life from which radicals are fleeing. The struggles of the student movement or the joys of the youth cultural revolution have had little direct bearing on the lives of housewives, and thus these nonfeminist movements have failed to earn their commitment.

The housewife constituency of the women's movement is in the mainstream of American life. Seldom have previous movements been able to gather constituents from within the so-called straight world of mundane responsibilities. The rebellion of youth during recent years struggled to establish a counterculture within which to nourish new institutions and relationships between persons. With comparable goals, women seeking to bring about changes within families cannot move to a new counterculture, for countless personal and institutional ties bind them to their present situation. The involvement of housewives in the women's movement not only makes this an *adult* movement but also opens the family and its place in society to the possibility of consciously directed changes.

The New Left Origins of the New Movement

FEMINISM AND THE NEW LEFT

The student and youth constituencies both of the new left and of the women's movement emerged after periods of quiescence and assumed what were considered by some as vanguard roles. The period of the 1950s, when American students were called a silent, apathetic generation, can be compared to the decades since 1920, when American women were considered the most favored and satisfied of their sex in the world. In reality the students of the fifties were expressing caution and suspended judgment as much as indifference; women, as has been stressed frequently in this text, spent the long years since female suffrage was granted in absorbing and assimilating the changes in all spheres of their lives, in education, jobs, social customs and institutions.

As the incidents of rebellion among women in the new left coalesced in the late 1960s into a new women's movement, many people saw the idea of women's liberation as the only hopeful sign on the American left. The new left, fragmented and at least temporarily in disarray, gave up its initial resistance and embraced feminism as its last rallying cry. The women's movement offered women *and* men on the left one last cause, one last renewal of theory and action for their political and personal lives. It may be hard to know, however, whether the emergence of the women's liberation movement signals the end of a period of new left activity or the start of a new series of liberation movements in society involving constituencies other than the familiar student and youth ones.

FEMINISM *VERSUS* THE NEW LEFT

The process by which women came into their own on the left shows the core of the ideas and ideals of the new women's movement.[2] The women's liberation issue remained submerged within the early new left. As America's war in Vietnam escalated and the black movement developed, the radical student movement grew and became more militant. Greater militance drew greater repression from the authorities. Young radicals began to see themselves as an oppressed class. SDS spokesman Carl Oglesby wrote:

[2] The preceding material on pages 129–132 on the women's movement and the new left appeared previously in Edith Hoshino Altbach, ed., *From Feminism to Liberation* (Cambridge, Mass.: Schenkman, 1971).

> *The new activists acquired their radical anti-authoritarianism*
> *at the end of police sticks. . . . The policeman's riot club*
> *functions like a magic wand under whose hard caress the*
> *banal soul grows vivid and the nameless recover their authen-*
> *ticity—a bestower, this wand, of the lost charisma of the*
> *modern self: I bleed, therefore, I am.*[3]

This male charisma and the set of attitudes and behavior it implied had become questionable, if not unacceptable, to many radical women by 1968. These women did not need to be hit over the head to become aware of themselves and others as oppressed beings. The day-to-day facts of male supremacy within the radical student movement and in the outside world began to fall into one pattern. Male leadership of the movement was increasingly experienced as male domination. Like the blacks before them, the women wanted a movement that would fight their own oppression.

RACISM AND SEXISM

The analogy between black oppression and women's oppression was of admitted inspiration to the women's movement. Women viewed the sexism that militates against them as related in kind if not in degree to the racism that keeps down blacks. Radical women saw a lesson in the fact that the black liberation movement seemed to come into its own when it split off from the racially integrated civil rights movement of the early sixties. (Black women, experiencing both racial and sexist op-pression, have begun to weigh the extent to which sexism could weaken their fight against the white man's racism, and out of all this much in-sight has been gained into the nature of oppression.)

The criticism has been raised that women's liberation as a movement is trying to coast in on the coattails of the black movement. The women's movement itself is gradually checking its defensive use of the analogy of the oppression of blacks and women, but in the early period that analogy was the beginning of a new consciousness on the left.

[3] Carl Oglesby, ed., *The New Left Reader* (New York: Grove Press, 1969), p. 15.

SEXISM AND THE ISSUE OF CLASS

Their new awareness as feminists provoked endless debate among women on the left. In question were not only the matters of priorities and first allegiance, whether to the general radical movement or to the women's movement above all else. All the basic ideas that these women had held as radicals were reexamined in the light of their new feminist consciousness. Furthermore, in the process of trying to sensitize the men on the left to their sexism, their chauvinistic behavior and attitude toward women, radical women developed deep and constructive criticisms of the male-dominated new left.

One of the most explosive issues to emerge from this reconsideration of radical tenets concerned attitudes toward social classes. Radical women analyzed the oppression of women and the oppression of the working class and the poor as stemming from the same attitudes—elitism and authoritarianism.[4] The women charged that the charismatic male theoreticians of the new left would never be able to relate to the working class if they could not even break out of their elitist attitudes toward their female comrades. Radical men felt superior to women in the way that the radical movement as a whole felt superior to the working class.

The authoritarian, coercive, and competitive character that the left has always condemned as part and parcel of a capitalistic ruling class bent on imperialism abroad and class exploitation and racism at home was located by radical women within the new left itself. The roles rewarded within the movement—those of guerrilla, street fighter, organizer, theoretician, and intellectual—were seen as roles society encourages in men and discourages in women. The Weathermen were accused, for example, of having accepted unquestioningly the most extreme image of masculinity that this brutalized society has to offer.

THE POLITICS OF CLASS MEETS THE POLITICS OF THE PERSONAL

Radical women moving away from the politics of the new left toward women's liberation attacked their male comrades on the level of personal life. As women ceased to accept setbacks in their personal lives as proof of individual failure, new patterns to their lives revealed themselves. The daily personal and even intimate trials in man-woman

[4] Kathy McAfee and Myrna Wood, "Bread and Roses," in Altbach, *From Feminism to Liberation*, pp. 21–38.

131

relationships were analyzed in terms of power politics. If the men dismissed personal problems as bourgeois whimpering—as men had long done on the American left—then, radical women were saying, they really knew very little about oppression. If the radical movement could not see oppression in the isolation, dependence, and denigration of women, how could they understand this psychological oppression among blacks or white-collar workers or assembly line workers or migrant workers? Women were bringing into doubt the entire collection of populist, anarchist, Marxist ideological fragments that the new left had picked up over a decade.

In view of the fact that some of the radical women pursuing this exposé of the new left had themselves been deeply involved in the movement, their criticisms were not only the indictment of a male-dominated movement but a self-indictment as well. Nor were the women alone in their criticism of the new left. Within the movement the work of Herbert Marcuse, Norman O. Brown, Wilhelm Reich, and others had opened up new possibilities toward the late 1960s. However, the new left was burning up its energies during the brief Weatherman period, and the works of these radical theoreticians received only a fraction of the attention they deserved. As for the women, the process of articulating their criticisms of the new left enabled them to start their own movement with some clarity of purpose—at least with an awareness of some mistakes to be avoided.

The Youth Culture

The confrontation with the new left was only part of the impetus for the women's liberation movement. In the late 1960s the political protest channeled through the organizations and demonstrations of the new left was gradually overshadowed by the daily cultural expression of dissent among youth. This youth culture, or counterculture, is not the only form of social or political movement that survived the decline of the new left, but it is the most pervasive new trend among teen-agers and young adults. The youth culture is also part of the milieu of the women's movement, and, as the years pass since the women's movement and the new left went their separate ways, many of the new left's political positions, disputed by feminists, have simply been absorbed in a diffuse and innocent way into the youth culture.

The message of "living the revolution," which the hippies celebrated and passed on to the whole youth culture, has been inherited by portions of the women's movement. Although the hippies and hip youth today do not see their life-styles in political terms, their decision to create to some degree their own institutions and morality here and now is very compatible with the women's movement's discovery that personal life is political. In the struggle against sexism, every man, woman, and child can represent the revolution. Personal life thereby becomes almost a legitimate political arena, not a haven where struggle can be laid aside. Thus the social and political meeting of the ideology of the new left and the life-style of the youth culture prepared the way for the women's movement.

However, the women's movement has not spared from a feminist critique the male-dominated communities of hippies and freaks. Sexism among men can continue to exist even after they let their hair grow long, adopt soft and colorful clothes, and cast off some of the accepted characteristics of masculinity in this society. As "chicks" and "old ladies" in the youth culture, women could be as effectively exploited and abused as in the straight world. Women willingly joined communes, but it did not remain unnoticed for long by the women's movement that within the anti-establishment framework of communal life male and female roles with regard to child rearing, sexuality, and housework fell into old established patterns. For many feminists the failure of the youth culture unequivocally to further the liberation of women from some of the dogmas of "femininity" raises doubts as to the liberating force of cultural dissent alone.

Conclusion

The women's movement possesses the rich heritage of dissent among students and youth of the sixties and the promise of a somewhat broader base thanks to the involvement of housewives on the one hand, and wage earners and professionals on the other. Although the women's movement is moving beyond the old constituencies of dissent, it still contains within itself almost the whole spectrum of ideology and strategy that the peace movement, the civil rights movement, the black power movement, the revolutionary youth movement, and the youth culture tried and, to some extent, discarded in the 1960s.

To chronicle the new left background of the new women's movement is to give but the historical context of its origins. As the movement reaches out toward new groups of women, it is rapidly outdistancing its political origins. Many veteran feminists, women in public office, industrial and professional workers, teen-agers, and housewives have no connection with the new left. These are the groups who will work to guide whatever direction the movement takes.

chapter 8

Day Care and the New Female Consciousness case study of a women's issue

A time of changing patterns in women's social lives produces individual issues each of which is the culmination of sometimes imperceptible developments in many spheres of life. In the 1960s and 1970s, for example, the outstanding women's issues, each arousing intense public discussion and action, have been the proposed Equal Rights Amendment to the Constitution (which would pertain to the status of women in labor, in education, and in the law), the rights of women on welfare, reforms in abortion law, and day care services.

The issue that shows perhaps most concretely the effects of some of the changing patterns in women's lives is day care—group child care services for preschool children. The question of day care illustrates the convoluted process by which a women's issue is raised in society and its resolution then becomes contingent upon changes in government, industry, the family, sex roles, and attitudes about parents and children. Because the issue of day care has lent itself to an immediate response, relatively speaking, it can serve as a current example of the broader implications of other issues concerning women.

Historical Overview

TRADITIONAL FORMS

The United States is not a country with a tradition of extensive day care programs. In this we are quite unlike many European countries, for example, where day care services have been available to the children of working mothers for many decades. In the American tradition, institutions for the group care of young children have until recently been all but restricted to charity for poor or nonfunctioning families and to emergency programs during times of war.

The pattern was set in the colonial period. To care for indigent children, religious orders in the Southern colonies founded infant schools, and in New England such children were commonly placed in foster homes or hired out as indentured servants. Until the nineteenth century most provisions for children whose parents were unable to take care of them were determined more by a desire for an orderly and economical solution to a social problem than by a deep concern for the needs of the family and of the child.

With the advent in the nineteenth century of a popular philosophy of human nature that singled out childhood as a unique and vital phase, educators and social commentators began to speak of the importance of the proper care and training of the children of working mothers. Mrs. Sarah Josepha Hale, editor of *Godey's Lady Book*, was an early supporter of infant schools where the children of both working and nonworking mothers could benefit from the care and instruction that their homes might not be able to provide to the same extent. A number of the utopian communities of the nineteenth century put into practice radical reforms in child-rearing methods.

However, except for scattered nurseries or infant schools with mixed enrollment, after the Civil War day care for children continued to be the work of welfare and charitable groups. Hospitals and settlement houses were the most common sponsors of such services. The annals of the Federation of Women's Clubs, for example, record that in the 1880s the Syracuse branch of the Women's Educational and Industrial Union had a day nursery for the children of working women.

The emergency labor situation that prevails during wartime has resulted in some special day care programs. In such periods, normally uninterested governmental and industrial bodies are swayed to set up day care centers to attract women into the war industries. During World War I, for example, day nurseries were set up at high schools in sections of Oakland, California. This arrangement freed high-school-aged children from baby-sitting at home for their younger siblings and gave the school curriculum a new practical subject—child care. During World War II the government again responded to the need for female labor by financing day care centers. At the height of the war approximately 130,000 children were being cared for in over three thousand centers. No more than 11 percent of the mothers in most war production areas were reported using the centers, and complaints of distressingly inadequate conditions and personnel were reported throughout the war. (It is questionable whether more working mothers would have used the centers even if government funding had been sufficient to cover the need for day care nationally.) Even these limited wartime day care programs were short-lived: funds for day care granted under the Lanham Act were cut off after the war.

OPPOSITION

Complementing the normal indifference of government and industry to day care services has been a body of opposition to the concept of group day care for young children. Among the middle class the opposition to day care has run deep; the middle class resisted for its own children what it condoned for the child victims of broken, impoverished homes.

There have been several sources for the resistance to day care. Since the nineteenth century the Old Guard fear has been that provisions for the care and nurture of young children outside the home would undermine the family. The existence of such provisions would, it was argued, also induce more women to leave the home and take up jobs. For children to spend most of their waking hours in infancy or young childhood away from the moral and spiritual influence of the home or homelike surroundings would not only interfere with the sacred bonds between parent and child but endanger the democratic rearing of children.

By the end of the nineteenth century most substantive proposals for change in the status of women or the family raised the specter of socialism or communism. The Old Guard feared that any collective rearing of children would lead to a totalitarian molding of character and values. This particular strain of opposition is in evidence even today in the arguments of some conservative legislators against recent proposals for federally funded day care. As the time drew near for the presidential acceptance or veto of a comprehensive federally funded program of day care in 1972, conservatives in Congress united to fight what they considered an anti-American development. Describing the proposals as a step toward a totalitarian, Nazi-like collectivized child raising, these latter-day critics of day care echoed the opponents of earlier periods.

The opposition of political conservatives has not, however, been in the mainstream of public resistance to the idea of day care. For many decades the rationale for resistance has come in the form of popularized theories on the traumatic effects upon the very young child of separation from its mother and, likewise, the danger of introducing any sort of mother-substitute.

Much of the expert opposition to day care is based on studies done after World War II on children in orphanages and war refugee camps. These children were deprived not only of the care and affection of their mothers but also of any human contact beyond the minimal custodial care. The emotional, mental, and physical retardation or abnormality that some of these children exhibited was then applied to situations in normal family life where the child is cared for by someone other than the mother during the day. In their most extreme interpretations, the theories were used to show how important it was that women devote full time to mothering their young children. For the working mother to leave her child in a day care center evoked in the public mind images of the deserted, neglected children of the wartime studies. Underneath all the theories, the expert critics of day care may have harbored the same fears for the integrity of the family as the political conservatives; the qualitative difference was that popular psychology became a more palatable and convincing way to resist any moves toward a collective solution to child care needs.

Child Care Needs

With all prospects blocked for an organized collective answer to the growing child care needs of working mothers, women have simply made individual arrangements for their preschool children. By 1965, one-fifth of all the nation's children under the age of fourteen (school-age children need child care after school hours) were in need of full-time or partial care because their mothers worked. Until the late 1960s, almost all these children were looked after by a relative or neighbor in a home; under 5 percent were cared for in a licensed day care center. It was estimated that several million children were in need of day care services.

The New Day Care Movement

Despite a tradition of marginal programs and the existence of a sizable body of opposition, the concept of day care has recently undergone a kind of rehabilitation. This new day care movement dates from about the mid-1960s and was accompanied by changes in the political, economic and educational evaluation of day care and by the new consciousness and changing social situation of women. Although these factors combined to alter the public attitude toward day care, they stemmed from divergent sectors and interest groups.

MOTIVATIONS OF GOVERNMENT

The federal government began a commitment to day care programs with the amended Social Security Act of 1967, which provided funds for day care services to the children of women on welfare. Through a maze of bureaucratic, legislative, and jurisdictional channels, the government was directing over $200,000,000 annually to day care programs by 1972. These funds were supporting over 250,000 children in licensed day care centers. While this beginning makes the familiar association of day care services with nominally protective social welfare policies, government's approach to day care in 1967 represented an entirely new evaluation of its political merits.

In the new frame of reference, government quite openly viewed day care as a positive tool in rehabilitating welfare families and integrating them into society. Programs such as Head Start were to adjust children of the poor and of racial minorities to the public school system through special preparation. The civil rights movement and a decade of rebellion in black communities had left the government groping for programs to stem the social and political unrest, and these seemed to be at least part of the answer.

In 1968, however, government policy on day care underwent a qualitative change. Since 1968, the federal government has remained only nominally interested in day care as a potential early socializer of deprived children. As official national priorities shifted from the eradication of poverty to the eradication of welfare rolls, day care for welfare children made budgetary common sense: establish day care centers, place welfare children in them, send welfare mothers out to work, thereby cutting welfare rolls. The Work Incentive Program (WIN), a voluntary work-training program for welfare mothers, initiated in

1968, was a step in this direction. The Nixon Family Assistance
Plan and several other welfare reform and day care proposals are all
indications that the government is working toward a welfare reform
measure with major provisions for day care services for the children of
welfare mothers. Recent changes in fee schedules in some jurisdictions
support the theory that government views day care as a new welfare
measure: in New York City an increase in the day care fees for all
children except those whose families are receiving public assistance is
having the effect of restricting day care service to welfare families.
Working parents in nonwelfare families, it appears, will be priced out
of the day care market.

MOTIVATIONS OF INDUSTRY AND BUSINESS

Government appreciation of the stabilizing potential of day care is
shared by the industrial community. This was illustrated by a day care
conference held in New York City in December of 1969. Assembled to
discuss the contribution that corporations could make to day care
services and the relevance of day care to corporate interests were rep-
resentatives from some of the largest corporations in the world: Con-
solidated Edison, Standard Oil, U.S. Steel, Bankers Trust, Chase Man-
hattan Bank, and United Fruit. The long-term relevance of day care
programs to corporate interests was specifically linked to the potential
of day care to forestall youth rebellion.

Early socialization of children in day care centers could, in the words
of the conferees, catch America's youth before they become dropouts,
hippies, and rebels and turn them into people who build up, not burn
down, buildings. In taking this position, the large corporations spoke as
government might in supporting programs of social action within the
system such as the Peace Corps, Junior Achievement, or the Job Corps.
The support for day care proclaimed at this and other, less select, local
conferences represents a basic change in policy on the part of management, which, in the past, preferred to ignore responsibility for the day
care needs of working parents.

In practice, of course, more substantive and immediate economic
benefits will determine whether employers of women all across the
nation will begin including day care services as one of their normal
operating procedures. Not just management in the innumerable textile
goods factories, insurance firms, and restaurants but even the federal
and state bureaucracies will want to assess whether providing day care

for the children of their female employees will attract responsible married women workers, cut job turnover and absenteeism, and increase productivity. Secondary benefits of reduced union militance and an overall improvement in worker-management relations would also be a consideration.

However, contrary to hearsay, rates of job turnover and absenteeism are not determined as much by sex as by occupational status. Occupations in the low-skill and low-paying categories have higher rates of turnover and absenteeism among both women and men than do the higher-grade occupations. In view of this, management in low-paying, low-skill jobs will want to assess whether day care would function to reduce labor costs among both their female and male workers.

If companies do stand to benefit from providing day care services to their employees, few companies have availed themselves of that technique. Moreover, in the period of several years during which the concept of day care has been undergoing a rehabilitation, no great spurt in company day care can be detected. The most immediate explanation for this is that the labor problems that management would presumably seek to solve through a day care program are not always as much of a drain on company profits as might be assumed. In the low-wage, low-skill jobs—which have the highest concentration of female workers—length of job tenure and continuity of work force are not as essential as they would be in technical or professional fields. Whether a worker stays on the job six months or six years, for instance, matters little in a job where it takes but one hour to train a new worker and one week for that new recruit to function as productively as the veteran. These are some of the reasons why all levels of industry and business cannot be expected, on their own, to launch day care programs. In the course of the 1970s, then, support and subsidy of day care from the private sector will depend upon the array of external pressures that is brought to bear upon employers.

ATTITUDES ON SOCIALIZATION

Raising the issue of day care implies a willingness to question the way children are socialized, the relationship between children and parents (especially mothers) and, ultimately, between families and educational institutions. It is hard to imagine the emergence of day care as an issue in the 1960s without the preceding period of popular and scientific discussion on early childhood development and education.

After World War II, while public discussion on early childhood development still centered on the need for consistent and continuous mothering, other research was gradually coming to the fore on the intellectual and social growth of infants and young children through a wealth of experiences. The revival of Maria Montessori's work and the application of Jean Piaget's theories were a part of these new trends.

The cumulative effect was to move the task of socializing children closer to science and farther away from instinctual parenthood. Emphasizing the centrality to a child's early well-being of cognitive learning and discovery among peers necessarily detracts from the old emphasis on the child's need for the protection and nurture of the full-time mother.

While treating child rearing as a science may cause some confusion and doubt among parents, it does open up new alternatives. It becomes permissible to envision positive supplements and even improvements to the care of children by one woman within the family circle. Parents become willing to entrust the early years of their children's lives to so-called experts or persons who can be trusted to provide experiences that the home may lack.

WOMEN'S CONSCIOUSNESS

If the new attitudes toward socialization were necessary to help turn the tide on the issue of day care, the last vital precondition for this altered appreciation of day care has been the new female consciousness. The basic shift occurring in the life patterns and commitments of American women affects how they view their responsibilities toward children. In exchange for their commitments outside the home that are beneficial to society (in the labor force or in higher education), women expect now to be relieved of some of the burden of responsibility for child care. This does not represent total delegation of responsibility; if anything it represents an attempt by parents to assert their control over the kind of care their children receive. Parents now feel freer to demand and expect day care services without the old sense of shame or failure because the family has turned to outsiders for help. Day care is being demanded as a family right.

As a part of the women's liberation movement, the issue of day care has many implications. Narrowly defined, day care has been an important demand for those in the women's movement who would liberate mothers from child care. In certain forms, this approach to day care as a women's issue can become as much antichild as it is prowoman. The demand for twenty-four-hour day care, for example, is the kind of demand that could not possibly be realized at this stage without hardship to the children.

More broadly defined, day care is an issue that allows some opportunity for practical application of the women's movement's vision of a nonsexist society. The emphasis is then not only on liberating women from child care but rather on including men and the community in general in the task. While day care will continue to be a women's issue for some time, this broader definition of the concept has shed new light on the relationship between children and their fathers, and between a society and its offspring.

Forms of Day Care

In 1967 licensed day care services were available to approximately 500,000 children in the United States. By 1969 that number had increased by 150,000, and by 1972 over 750,000 children were receiving care in licensed group child care centers. Since 1968 licensing bureaus have been hard-pressed in the large urban areas to keep up with applications for licenses for new centers.

The new day care movement has several crosscurrents. In view of the variety of supporters, subsidizers, and users of the services, this is not surprising. In order to appreciate these differences, it will be useful to group the kinds of centers according to the community served and the mode of financing. The boundaries between categories are not rigid, of course, and, needless to say, much overlapping and shifting occurs in the lifetime of any center.

Three broad categories can be discerned: institutional and industrial centers, profit-based centers, and community centers.

INSTITUTIONAL AND INDUSTRIAL CENTERS

These are centers established for the children of employees of one particular institution or company. The center is usually located in the place of work itself (within, for example, the hospital or factory) or in an adjacent building. It is usually subsidized to a great extent or entirely by the company. The company hires the staff and provides the facilities. The parents pay a token fee or one that varies according to income. Parent involvement in the decisions concerning staff and program at the

143

center are minimal, since in the few industrial centers and in the hundred or so hospital centers the initiative has come from the company. Moreover, under present circumstances, it would be difficult for the employee-parent to take a critical stance regarding the center. Reliable day care is hard to find, much less day care easily accessible from the parent's place of work, and, consequently, employees would think many times before voicing a complaint that might place in jeopardy the privilege of using the day care center. Thus far, then, industrial and institutional day care is treated by both management and employees as a bonus service provided by the good will of the company.

Labor unions have for some time now placed the demand for day care services very high on their list of priorities. Day care centers founded by unions themselves were even a rarer occurrence prior to the 1960s than employer-established centers. Only a few unions—typically in the predominantly female needle trades—formed centers for their membership. Yet, such centers may provide a future alternative model for industrial and institutional day care. Such centers would be founded and maintained by the union, with funding by the companies or institutions whose employees would use the service. Union management would be one way to ensure the opportunity for parent participation in planning the kind of care their children would receive.

A situation in which working parents are dependent for day care services upon the very powers that control their jobs is one that invites abuse. The circumstances can be imagined in which admission to the day care center would be decided on the basis of employee good behavior or other criteria harmful to the independence and integrity of the worker. Thus, as day care for employees expands, as it surely will, to meet the growing demand, the question of control of day care centers will become increasingly important.

The main obstacle to the provision of institutional and industrial day care services is the unwillingness of companies, universities, and hospitals to make the necessary investment in money, space, planning, and administration that the services require. Existing inducements—parent demand, tax deductions, and the possibility of federal assistance—have not yet overcome the resistance of management.

PROFIT-BASED CENTERS

Inevitably, in the wake of any social movement with investment potential, entrepreneurs will enter the field. The day care movement is no exception: although profit-based day care centers are a marginal part of the movement, both individual profit-based centers and franchise chains will continue to expand with the day care market.

Every year hundreds of new small businesses, both licensed and unlicensed, that deal in day care come and go. In storefronts, in apartments, and in basements, day care businesses are set up, with minimal budgets, personnel, materials, meals, programs, and facilities. In many cases the entrepreneurs are women family heads who are attempting to turn a lifetime of experience in baby-sitting into a viable source of income. In this twilight zone of the day care movement desperate working parents leave their children in the care of almost equally desperate shopkeepers, both struggling to keep income ahead of debts.

The distinction must be made between custodial day care and quality day care. The stark fact is, however, that no profits can be made from quality day care centers. Every local and national survey has reported the same findings: quality day care costs about twice as much per week per child as the profit-based center can charge parents. Private profit-based day care enterprises are not eligible for federal, state, or private foundation funds. Therefore, in the end, the children are the ones who pay the price—in boredom and in mental, emotional, and physical suffering. As federal, state, and county day care standards are clarified and made enforceable, the individual profit-based centers will be the first to feel the pressure.

Franchise day care center chains are another story. Because they have at their disposal national corporative resources, franchise day care centers may have a greater longevity than the small day care operations. Mass produced in professional-looking prefabricated packages, franchise day care has a bright and cheerful exterior that nevertheless masks the familiar abuses. For example, franchise day care is less open to parental control than any other form of day care service.

The future of both kinds of profit-based day care centers depends on the extent to which supporters of day care can extract local and federal funds so as to upgrade the quality of day care services. Once that occurs, all but the most conscientious, dedicated, and well-run profit-based centers (still, unfortunately, unable to make a profit from quality programs) will be unable to survive.

COMMUNITY CENTERS

Community centers are the grass roots and vanguard of the new day care movement. These are nonprofit centers that admit children from the community—community being defined as anywhere from the surrounding area to the immediate neighborhood. Community centers are not self-supporting and must be subsidized, but they have little more in common than this basic financial reality. Modes of financing, forms of sponsorship, specifics of philosophy, goals, and atmosphere in the centers are as various as are the participants.

Beginnings Community centers have every kind of beginning. Some are cooperative neighborhood ventures by a group of parents who share a common need for day care. Other centers have been organized by the combined efforts of any number of interested parties: prominent civic-minded citizens, charity groups, Vista volunteers, or possibly a group of active Head Start mothers. (Head Start day care centers, now largely defunct, were perhaps the first of the community centers in the new movement.) Still other community centers are run under the auspices of the Salvation Army or individual church groups or are neighborhood house centers that have been rejuvenated by the new day care movement. Most of the federally supported day care programs initiated since the late 1960s, in fact, were begun in one of these ways.

The immediate and continual crisis that all community centers face is one of financing. Subsidies can come in the form of donated space, equipment, cheap rental property, volunteer or student-intern staff members; centers accept anything and everything while they discover what works best for them. Fund raising is a complex art, for the money must be extracted from a myriad of sources through a labyrinth of channels, some mutually exclusive or conflicting. As a result, each community day care center has a lively tale to tell in the history of its own struggle into existence.

Future Challenges The task of sustaining quality day care programs is a continuing problem for any center, but particularly so for community centers. Federal and state funds are often sufficient only to launch a center through its early period and provide the bare essentials in materials and staff. Centers wishing to experiment in new programs, however, or seeking to acquire more equipment and a larger staff do not find easy

146

funding. People working to provide quality day care with parent and community involvement are being forced to the conclusion that federal and other funding agencies are interested only in *custodial care*. Therefore, in order to build the kinds of programs they envision, community day care people must personally subsidize the programs. Overtime without pay is standard practice: preparations, meetings among staff or with parents, and attention to administrative details can consume many hours of overtime.

The single most essential prerequisite for creative day care is a good staff-to-children ratio. Yet, it is often impossible to obtain funds for new staff members. Because of stipulations attached to federal and local funding, it is often easier to obtain money for every possible kind of appliance from dishwasher to color television than for salaried staff. Volunteers from among parents and friends of the center can only partially meet the need. Therefore, time and time again dedicated staff members accept salary cuts and in this way subsidize good programs.

The result is that the demands of the job in time and energy can become intolerable, leading to a high turnover rate in day care staff. Nor is this problem avoided in parent cooperative centers; if anything, the problem is exacerbated because parents in cooperative day care usually have the combined responsibilities of outside paid employment, day care tasks, and family duties. It could happen that insufficiently funded day care programs could re-create in group form the oppressive situation of the harassed mother caring for her children all day every day.

Day care owes its existence to the growing awareness of communal responsibility in the raising of children in their youngest years. However, unless public and private funds are released for this socially significant labor, quality day care will continue to require a calculated sacrifice on the part of day care workers.

Conclusion

As the new day care movement grows, it will continue to send out shock waves through society. As a women's issue it signals a new approach to the amelioration of women's lives and may have as yet unforseen repercussions on women's position in the home and in the labor force.

With the exception of periods during the nineteenth-century woman movement, the intent of most discussion on women's issues has centered on the assumed female need for protection. Protective labor legislation, the prime example of enlightened reform in the Pre-World War I Progessive Era, was based on a concept of the weakness of the female sex. Women workers would always occupy a precarious position in the labor force, it was felt, because childbearing and the responsibilities of home and family were such an inescapable drain on their health, time, and energy. Furthermore, the demands of their dual roles as workers and housewives and their supposed unsuitability as organizers were given as reasons why they would not be able to fight for self-protection through labor unions.

The new female consciousness seeks instead to pinpoint more basic contributing factors to women's vulnerable, and inferior, status in society. The individual demands for birth control, abortion, day care, and rights in all fields of endeavor will replace the mantel of legal protection upon which women have been forced to rely in past periods. These issues and the conditions and consciousness that have brought them to the fore signify profound changes in the situation of men, children, *and* women in American society.

chapter 9

The New Women's Movement
dynamics and prospects

As the women's movement moved swiftly away from its new left connections, ideological diversity was followed by organizational diversity. In the place of the new left's handful of national organizations, each with a particular, if not always well defined, political position, the women's movement sustains many groups, many issues, many positions and strategies. The new left, in the course of its history, also tried a series of positions and strategies, but transitions were made in stages; sit-ins, mass peace marches, community organizing, street fighting were tried in sequence. The women's movement, on the other hand, pursues its various courses of action simultaneously.

Diversity of Organization

Nothing so clearly differentiates this women's movement from the recent new left and from the previous feminist movement as its lack of, and lack of desire for, all-embracing organizations. Organizations do exist that function with a national office and a full complement of regional chapters: they represent the growing sense of common purpose among women in professional fields and in public life. The most active of these organizations is the National Organization of Women (NOW); among the more recently founded are the Women's Equity Action League (WEAL) and the National Women's Political Caucus.

Nevertheless, large organizations, regional or national, that represent a particular political position do not set the tone or the style of this movement, although the possibility does, of course, exist that at some future time unifying organizations within the women's movement and perhaps even new political parties may evolve.

Feminism has caused women to question not only the ideology but also the strategy of the new left. For women who came up through the ranks of the new left, political organizations are associated with scenes of elitism, authoritarianism, and sectarianism; women were intimidated by the habit the new left fostered of judging people by their political credentials. Since this in-fighting within the new left hampered the work of the movement and oppressed women as well, women from this background are now hesitant to create organizations within which one group of women might exclude or ostracize another group because of supposed differences in ideology or strategy. What remains is a debate within the women's movement on what kind of structure is necessary in order to sustain the solidarity of sisterhood while the work of the movement is done.

INDIVIDUAL WOMEN'S GROUPS

The anonymity, even obscurity, of the majority of women's groups is a fact that escapes the mass media, centered as they are in the large urban centers—and mainly in New York City, where such groups tend to be more vocal, and more publicity conscious. Perhaps because of the concentration of media in New York, that city's women's groups seem to produce more position papers and articles than those in any of the other cities combined. These publications are then disseminated through the land, and anyone wishing to write about the state of the women's movement inevitably ends up with more material about its activities in New York City than anywhere else. However, New York City and its major organizations—Radical Feminists, Redstockings, and WITCH (Women's International Terrorist Conspiracy from Hell)—are not typical of the women's liberation movement.

Groups in the women's liberation movement fall into three categories: personal discussion, study, and project groups. They may choose for themselves, however, a wide variety of designations—caucus, union, collective, brigade, cell, or, simply, group. Membership in any given group may be either mixed or limited to women whose primary identification is as socialist, academic, married, single, divorced, or lesbian women. Many of these groups are not mutually exclusive, thus allowing members to belong to several at the same time. Moreover, in a short span of time one women's group may, through changes in its membership or the emergence of a new need or interest, shift its emphasis from study to personal discussion or undergo any number of splits and permutations. These three types of small groups, however, remain the basic unit of the women's movement.

The Spectrum of Political Viewpoints   The flexibility and openness suggested by the diversity encompassed by the women's movement has not, however, eradicated incompatibilities and hostilities among the groups. The pluralism of the women's movement means not that its members accept all tendencies but rather that the issue of women's liberation can draw support from women of quite divergent political persuasions.

At one end are women who would agree with the slogan from the American Socialist Party prior to World War I: "The Socialist who is not a Feminist lacks breadth, and the Feminist who is not a Socialist is lacking in strategy." At the other end (and here the terms right and left wing have lost their meaning) are radical feminists for whom socialism is almost irrelevant to feminism; in their view a socialist revolution would leave undisturbed the sexism rooted in human relationships and institutions. Around each of these poles in the movement are clusters of groups that may gravitate toward one or the other position but basically shun any political designation and focus instead on a particular issue—e.g., abortion, day care, welfare rights.

The coexistence of such an array of tendencies within the women's movement has raised the question of political irresponsibility in the minds of some women (feminists of varying persuasions) and probably many radical men. At issue is whether the potential of women's liberation as a mass movement is being blunted or even sabotaged by the presence of women with a middle-class and liberal perspective and by the concentration of many groups on personal consciousness raising. (It should be remembered, though, that criticism of attention to personal issues has been raised in many a radical movement.)

Personal Consciousness Raising   Attitudes within the women's movement on consciousness raising through discussion of personal relationships in women's lives have undergone a reversal within a few short years. Responding to their new left training, some women had resisted the new mandate to share feelings and discover with a group of women what it meant to be female in this society. To those who considered themselves revolutionary socialists, attention to personal life sounded rather like a middle-class luxury. This attitude persisted for several years, even after the women's movement had been accepted as a cause by the left. Consciousness raising was fully accepted only after radical women realized that their women's group lost cohesion and energy by refusing to allow personal feelings to enter their "political" discussions.

Soon women's study and project groups were including personal consciousness raising in their meetings, sometimes stopping the business at hand to work out personal problems a woman was facing or to improve communication and trust among the women in the group. A group whose purpose was to concentrate on academia might, after several months of studying reports and statistics, feel the need to backtrack and spend a number of meetings on personal revelations and supportive discussions. Sharing experiences and understanding among a group of women thus became a valid and accepted part of the women's movement.

CONFERENCES

In a way seldom seen in social and political movements, the constituents of the women's movement are self-organized. The absence of national umbrella organizations and the diversity of small groups results in almost total autonomy for individual women's associations. Counterbalancing this multiplicity of discrete units, however, are local or regional women's conferences.

Women's conferences offer women in the same region or town the chance to meet, exchange information, develop their thinking on certain issues, and form new groups. The conferences are usually planned by a coalition of groups that forms an ad hoc committee to schedule the workshops and arrange for the speakers, the literature, the meals, the meeting place, and other accommodations. There are no officers to elect or list of points to be approved, and much of the work of the conference takes place in the workshops, which reflect the major issues of the movement—marriage, family, sexuality, abortion, the law, jobs, the political economy of sexism, and other theoretical and practical topics.

These conferences bear little resemblance to the conventions of the increasingly factionalized new left in the late 1960s. If comparisons to recent movements are in order, we might say that women's conferences recall those of the early peace movement, circa 1959–1961. Women's conferences have older feminists in attendance along with young activists, much as the peace movement in its early stages brought together veteran pacifists, old leftists, and young radicals. And the sessions of personal consciousness raising at women's conferences resemble the old pacifist workshops on nonviolence.

Women's conferences are not arenas for grand ideological and bureaucratic confrontation. The lines have not yet been so sharply drawn. Rather, these small local or regional conferences offer the movement a way to bridge the isolation of the small groups, rendering less abstract the sense of solidarity and sisterhood that feminism, at least in some measure, creates and, in general, suiting the women's movement well in its free-form period.

WOMEN'S CENTERS

What conferences can accomplish for a few days, women's centers may perpetuate. The centers can provide a meeting ground for women whose lives might not otherwise overlap and can give women a place of their own: a place where services can be offered, where work groups can meet, where classes can be held, and where women who need to can take refuge, at least temporarily, while coming to terms with their own lives. Ideally, the new centers could combine the functions of the old neighborhood stores and taverns, the local library, welfare refuge homes, and adult education and vocational training schools. Here women might be comforted, organized, taught, counseled, fed and housed, as the need arose. Beyond providing such services, which is itself a major motivation behind the centers, they can serve, as do the women's conferences, to give more tangible evidence of sisterhood throughout the female community.

As small neighborhood stores go under, undone increasingly by the giant shopping centers on the outskirts of towns, empty storefront real estate attracts new entrepreneurs and missionaries. In among the old charitable rummage stores and diners strange new establishments spring up—natural food shops, weaving and sewing co-ops, day care centers, and, now, women's centers. Leaving the protective and restrictive confines of university environs, women's centers are moving out into residential and small-business neighborhoods, where they sense their new constituents will be. As they move out into the community, these centers become the vanguard of the women's movement, carrying forward and broadening its progress.

Unresolved Issues

So far we have described the women's movement on its own terms in an effort to catch its total spirit and dynamic. Certain unresolved problems, however, become apparent, even to the most sympathetic and committed observer, as they have, indeed, in many cases, to those within the women's movement itself.

FREE FORM

Inasmuch as the women's liberation movement is a broad-base social movement with varied constituencies, the diversity of organization is understandable. This means that the openness in structure cannot be claimed by the movement to be the result of a calculated and directed political *strategy*. Indeed, no social movement that arises from the cultural, social, and economic experience of society can claim a well-articulated strategy—especially in its early stage. Women may look at the diversity they have in the movement and seek to use it to advantage, but this is a different matter. Likewise, the observation that the forms of organization are often responses to various impulses and inclinations and to paths of least resistance, and the movement's commitment to respect the integrity of these forms, has come after the initial fact of diversity.

Unless checked, however, free-form organization could lead to the diffusion and thus the weakening of the women's movement. Without the resources and discipline of ongoing organizations to coordinate efforts, the movement will lack consistency, continuity, and depth. It has occurred to women in the movement that each new year brings new faces but few innovations in the analysis of women's problems or the program to resolve them. There comes a point at which it is not sufficient for a movement to be growing only in numbers. In order to hold its members a movement must offer them the means and the hope to understand their lives and society and to gain control over both. The militant women who left the Socialist Party before World War I never found the alternative organizational form in which to unite their socialist and feminist convictions. The same diffusion of the feminist spirit, as it searches for effective organizational forms, could occur again in the 1970s.

POLITICS OF THE PERSONAL

The emergence of the politics of the personal—an acceptance of the validity of exploring personal experiences and reactions—has brought about a positive change in the lives of many women. The question is, At what point does personal consciousness raising cease to be illuminating and become self-defeating, even self-indulgent? The content of women's groups that focus on personal discussion does run the risk of becoming circular. The discontent and the conflicts individual women express become perpetuated as group experience. A group of women can gain in understanding and empathy, but sitting around in weekly meetings does not change the conditions that caused the discontent or the conflicts. Politics involves gaining control. When a strategy or tactic ceases to help people take control of their lives, it also ceases to be political.

Many women in the movement have gone from group to group, searching for compatible women with whom to form the intimacy required for personal sharing. If each unit of ongoing work in the movement—be that work the fostering of personal awareness on the part of individual women or the establishment of services and counterinstitutions—is dependent on the whim of a small group of women, there can be little progress.

A backlash of sorts is in progress within the movement against the politics of the personal. The reaction has come not so much from socialist women as from women who believe that the time to struggle toward a feminist revolution is at hand. These critics decry the inordinate amount of time and energy spent in struggling to liberate women in their personal relationships with men and children. They question whether women have the right to a personal life now if they are truly dedicated to feminism. Let women learn the discipline of revolutionary guerrillas, they say, who can live without the opposite sex and their families for years at a time. Perhaps this backlash is the prelude to a separatist trend within the movement; at the very least, the reaction against personal politics, if it spreads, should bring about a change in the movement's composition.

IDEAS VERSUS IDEOLOGY

The almost astounding sense of solidarity among women that the women's movement fosters had no equal during any of the phases of

155

the new left. In the student-based new left movement, students or other youth outside the movement were often dismissed or attacked as scabs, jocks, pigs, fascists, and reactionaries, or else they were simply ignored. The new left seemed to be saying to its contemporaries, Either you are with us or you are against us. In the women's movement there is in many quarters the need to say, Even if you aren't ready for us, we are still with you, sisters. The point is not that there is no dissension among women or that women do not call each other scabs and oppressors on occasion, but rather that a general mandate of solidarity among sisters envelops the movement.

The solidarity of sisterhood can cover a multitude of ideas and positions that may not combine to form a coordinated strategy or an ideology. The doctrine of sisterhood can cause the movement to deny the conflicts and inconsistencies within its positions. To expose these conflicts and to develop a consistent ideology necessitates stepping out, judging women, allowing some leaders to come forth. Perhaps the concept of sisterhood is still too new for this generation of feminists to put it into jeopardy.

Consequently, the women's movement is allowing some potentially divisive, but crucial, issues to remain at the rhetorical level. The issue of class is one example.

To proclaim the sisterhood of women and to discover that the oppression of the sex crosses class lines are the beginnings in the liberation of women from the class isolation that divides them. However, the women's movement, with its middle-class moorings, has tended to interpret women's oppression in terms of being denied positions of responsibility and respect, being confined to the home, and being treated as a sex object. A woman with twenty years' experience as a waitress or on the assembly line may consider a secretarial job as an unattainable privilege. Moreover, a working-class woman, neither trained for nor socialized to relish the competitiveness and ambition involved in a career, may even long for a respite from the labor force. A woman forced by poverty to farm out her children to foster families may well long for the family and home that her middle-class counterpart finds so confining.

Socialist women who came from the new left into the women's movement have stressed that the oppression of women takes different forms, according to class. For this they have on occasion been attacked by other feminists as being divisive, as having been subverted by male dogmas—i.e., Marxism. So they often retreat to rhetoric. However, socialist women do not serve working-class women better when they reduce the class issue to

156

a slogan. Statements such as "Women's economic function is to repro-
duce and maintain the labor force," while true in a historical sense, make
a mockery of many women's lives. Moreover, such statements hark back
to a previous century of Marxist ideology and are relatively useless in
fashioning an ideology and strategy for the women's movement in this
society.

The most effective check to the weak points in feminist ideology and
organization would be the development of the new constituencies of
housewives and wage-earning women. Such constituents can bring a
workday realism and responsibility to the ideas and programs of the
women's movement that will carry them beyond the level of rhetoric.
The trend toward the establishment of community counterinstitutions
and services—not only those that are primarily feminist ventures—could
do much to deepen the range of the women's movement.

Mass Media and the Movement Image

The ease with which trends in society are elevated to the state of full-
blown movements prompts one to question the effect of the media on
the women's movement. Looking back over the last ten years, during
which the civil rights, black power, peace, student, and youth movements arose, one finds that the initial trial period grows ever shorter.
That period when a social trend may coalesce and solidify in obscurity
is a luxury no longer possible. Instead, the trend quickly attracts the
exhilarating attentions of press, radio, and television. But then, as with
the major social movements of the 1960s, it becomes the puppet of the
media, alternately courted and condemned. Thus, in addition to external or internal substantive problems, all the movements of the recent
past have had to face an addition threat—the powerful effects of the
media.

The seductiveness of the mass media cannot create movements where
no support exists, but the media can pace movements and determine
directions. Aided and abetted by news reports, isolated demonstrations
or statements by women's groups have been magnified and followed
closely by press conferences and the emergence of new leaders, organizations, and women's journals. Enlarged to national proportions at a time
when its base was more local in scope, the women's movement has spent
much time during its first years trying to act as if it *were* a national
movement.

Not only can the media catapult a trend into a national movement while it is still in its infancy, but they can overplay a movement so that it seems old before its time. The sensationalizing of issues can accelerate or provoke the advent of a backlash in public opinion. By 1972, women's liberation had been an issue in the United States for about four years—a short time in feminist history, but a long time in the memory of the news establishment, ever on the search for new feature stories. The issues raised by the women's liberation movement became reduced to "that women's lib thing." Three years into the current women's movement one could read in major newspapers that the movement had failed because women interviewed in a few small towns—in factories or on farms—had reacted negatively to it. However, in the kind of irony that results from manipulative reporting, the women were actually reacting to features of the women's movement that had been dramatized and magnified by the media—like the bra-burning issue.[1]

Yet, a discussion of the relationship of the women's movement to the mass media cannot be solely an indictment of press, radio, and TV. Some women themselves are responsible for the movement's distorted image in the media. Perhaps because the media are so much a part of daily life, women in the movement have consciously and unconsciously tailored their ideas and programs to be media-exploitable. Certainly women in the movement have themselves been dismayed to view the media-determined scenarios of demonstrations, press conferences, and talk show appearances by movement figures, and so forth.

Although 1972 brought women's liberation as an issue to the Democratic National Convention, the movement seems headed, for the present at least, toward a retrenchment, as it steps back from the limelight to reassess its situation.

Conclusion

The configuration of changes that made a women's liberation movement possible in the 1960s can be interpreted as the bankruptcy of the attitude of reliance on women's individual endeavor. Groups of women now hesitate before explaining their condition on the job, in school or elsewhere as the result solely of personal success or failure. Changes in every sphere of

---

[1] Judy Klemesrud, "In Small Town U.S.A., Women's Liberation Is Either a Joke or a Bore." *The New York Times* (March 22, 1972), p. 54.

women's lives have replaced the personal view with a collective one and have brought about a fundamental reassessment of women.

What are the roots of this new feminism of the 1960s and 1970s? One temptation is to see the women's liberation movement as part of a pattern of social disintegration. If not wholly that, the movement is still certainly much more than just the latest permutation of the youth movement or counterculture. At the very least, we can say it is not surprising that a movement of women appeared, given the following developments:

The rise in women's labor force participation
Their concentration in service and white-collar occupations
The drop in percentage of women in the professions
The increase in employment of married women and, specifically, of mothers
The crisis in the situation of women on welfare
The drop in marriage and birth rates
The so-called sexual revolution
The rise in crimes commited by and against women
The dramatic rise in rapes in particular
The abuse of women in the mass media

Given all these things and many more, it is easy to see why some groups of women would demand changes. However, as many of these given conditions are long-standing ones, or, at any rate, part of an accelerating trend whose origins extend back beyond the recent past, it is not yet clear why the late 1960s in particular were the years to spawn a feminist revival.

Perhaps the changes in women's lives, and their growing disillusionment with their roles, offer some clues to the current upheaval in feminist consciousness. The prosperous and antifeminist period ushered in with the close of World War II was one in which the domestic roles of women were infused with an unparalleled romanticism even as their economic and social functions became ever more marginal. Even as the romanticization of femininine roles was occurring, the prosperity that made that possible was ironically undermining those very roles.

Isolation and versatility have been characteristics of women's lives in the modern period, with isolation increasing as the varied responsibilities of the feminine role were separated from recognized productive work, as we have chronicled above. In the period following World War II economic factors seriously altered these aspects of women's roles. Initially, the national prosperity created new jobs and expanded old occupations to draw more women into the labor force. However from the late 1950s on, pockets of economic instability have forced unemployment and cost of living figures up; this, in turn, forced women—particularly married women—to seek employment who otherwise might not have entered the labor force. Not only have the exclusive images of home and family as havens of security and fulfillment been tarnished, but women's self-image and public image have undergone shifts.

Fewer women now expect to spend most of their adult lives isolated at home. Once they have entered the labor force, even on a part-time or sporadic basis, women no longer feel as obliged or able to absorb all the varied responsibilities that they used to without remuneration or recognition. This has resulted in pressure from women to change the institution of marriage—revealed in the rising incidence of divorces initiated by the wife, new sexual demands, as well as a variety of demands for social legislation and services in the areas of welfare rights, child care, abortion law reforms, etc.

Most women know best domestic life and its work—both what we have called the blue- and white-collar functions. However, women have also come to be very familiar with all areas of the labor force—part-time and volunteer work as well as full-time industrial service, white collar, and professional jobs. Often women have no choice as to their work, but increasingly they are realizing that the rewards are not worth the juggling act required to keep up in their many roles. As years go by, the word spreads of the low repute of unpaid labor, of discriminations in pay and advancement on the job, of sexual favors demanded and extracted in the outside world and of many other indignities awaiting women. All the options have been tested. More women now know the hoax of salvation through domestic tranquility, through a job or a career, through spinsterhood or the sexual revolution, or through simply a higher standard of living.

Women's renewed feminist consciousness, it can be argued, stemmed from decades of tokenism and individual struggle. Human consciousness, it appears, takes leaps of recognition, and in the decade of the 1960s groups of American women took that leap of consciousness and became feminists. Perhaps this process is but the self-destructive mechanism of a pluralistic society. The fact remains, nonetheless, that people are offered an endless series of solutions on a personal basis, alternatives that hold out the rewards of security, fulfillment, and joy. When none of these work, people begin to question some of the premises upon which the solutions are based. Women have begun to question what it means to be a woman in this society.

APPENDIX

Events of Note in
The History of American Women

Date	Employment, Technology, Inventions, Health, Home, Morals, Fashion, Education	Achievements and Events, Woman Movement, Women's Liberation Movement, and Miscellaneous
1617	Marriageable women begin arriving in Virginia for sale to planters.	
1619	First slaves land at Virginia.	
1623	Women and children arrive in New England to join husbands and fathers.	
1627	1,500 children, kidnapped in Europe, arrive in Virginia to become servants and laborers.	
1636	Massachusetts requires single persons to live in families. Harvard College founded.	
1638		Anne Hutchinson, charged, condemned, and banished as a heretic by the Massachusetts ecclesiastical synod.

Date	Employment, Technology, Inventions, Health, Home, Morals, Fashion, Education	Achievements and Events, Woman Movement, Women's Liberation Movement, and Miscellaneous
1639		Margaret Brent makes unsuccessful request for the right to vote in the Maryland Assembly.
1641	In Plymouth children of relief recipients are legally required to work.	
1647	Rhode Island law declares marriage by mutual agreement illegal. Massachusetts requires its towns to maintain schoolmasters.	Margaret Brent begins a campaign for the vote after being refused this right by the Maryland Assembly.
1648		Margaret Jones becomes first witch executed in the Salem, Mass. witch-hunt.
1649–1660	Puritan enforcement of moral conduct becomes rigid.	
1650		Publication in London of *The Tenth Muse* by New England's first poet, Anne Bradstreet.
1651	New Haven court upholds the indenturing of children without the father's consent. Sale of toys and dolls in the stores of Boston and Salem indicates softening of views toward childhood.	
1655	Illiteracy of women is estimated at about 50%.	

Date	Employment, Technology, Inventions, Health, Home, Morals, Fashion, Education	Achievements and Events, Woman Movement, Women's Liberation Movement, and Miscellaneous
1656		First all-woman jury in the colonies acquits woman accused of infanticide—she claimed she was never even pregnant.
1660	Connecticut law requires married men to live with their wives. Massachusetts holds men proved to be fathers of bastards liable for child support. Divorce granted a woman in Delaware from husband she charged was an adulterer and had beaten her. South Carolina advertisement in England promises women "a golden age" in the colonies.	
1662	Virginia establishes inheritance of slave status through the mother.	
1663	Man charged with wife trading is punished.	
1670	Boston woman is licensed to sell coffee and chocolate, thus beginning coffeehouse tradition in U.S.	
1678		*Several Poems Compiled with Great Variety of Wit and Learning,* by Anne Bradstreet—first book of poems by a woman published in colonies.

Date	Employment, Technology, Inventions, Health, Home, Morals, Fashion, Education	Achievements and Events, Woman Movement, Women's Liberation Movement, and Miscellaneous
1691		Ducking stool, common form of female punishment in the South, built in front of New York city hall, for the punishment of scolds.
1692–1693	College of William and Mary chartered.	Salem witch-hunt—by 1693, 20 witches had been executed; 2 died in prison.
1693	John Locke writes *Some Thoughts Concerning Education*, which becomes influential in rearing of children in America.	
1700s	Extravagant dress of colonial period includes high heels, stiff stays, and large curled wigs for men and women.	
1701		Status of colonial women shown by fact that 6 women sat in a jury on special duty in Albany.
1705	Virginia requires children of white women and Negro men to serve as slaves for 31 years.	
1709–1710	3,000 German immigrants arrive in New York.	
1719	Approximate date of first publication of *Mother Goose's Melodies for Children*.	
1725		First known scalping of Indians by white men—in New Hampshire.

Date	Employment, Technology, Inventions, Health, Home, Morals, Fashion, Education	Achievements and Events, Woman Movement, Women's Liberation Movement, and Miscellaneous
1734	Benjamin Franklin: "Where there's marriage without love, there will be love without marriage."	
1735		Increased wealth allows more women to leave husbands, live independently. Newspapers carry accounts of runaway wives and elopements.
1739–1744		Eliza Lucas Pinckney experiments successfully in indigo production.
1742	"Franklin stove" invented by Benjamin Franklin.	
1745	Whist becomes popular game for ladies and gentlemen together.	
1746	First boarding school for girls founded in Bethlehem, Pa., by Moravian settlers.	
1750s		Custom of sending valentines begins.
1759		Phillis Wheatley sold in Boston slave market; she later becomes published poet, visits court in London.
1760s	Stoves for heat and cooking become more common.	
1761		Mrs. E. Smith edits *The Complete Housewife or Accomplished Gentlewoman's Companion,* one of earliest American cookbooks.

Date	Employment, Technology, Inventions, Health, Home, Morals, Fashion, Education	Achievements and Events, Woman Movement, Women's Liberation Movement, and Miscellaneous
1765	Advertisement by Philadelphia teacher promises to teach ladies to spell and to point with propriety, without hindering their eligibility for matrimony.	
1770s	"Tower" reappears as popular hairstyle for rich women—high-piled, greased, and powdered curls with jewels.	
1770		Boston women organize tea boycott.
1770–1790		Judith Murray writes articles on woman's rights.
1773	Stiff girdling of females comes into style.	
1774		Ann Lee, "Mother Ann," arrives in New England, forms Shaker sect.
1775		Tom Paine writes on subservient position of women.
1776		New Jersey becomes first colony to grant woman suffrage; statute reversed 1807.
1777		In letter, Abigail Adams admonishes husband to remember the rights of women.
1784	First magazine aimed at women as well as men: *Gentlemen and Ladies Town and Country Magazine,* Boston.	Phillis Wheatley dies penniless in Boston.
1785	Bundling custom falls into disrepute, because of better heating of homes and new etiquette.	

Date	Employment, Technology, Inventions, Health, Home, Morals, Fashion, Education	Achievements and Events, Woman Movement, Women's Liberation Movement, and Miscellaneous
1790	Textile mill built in Pawtucket by Samuel Slater.	
1791	Alexander Hamilton recommends employment of women and children in manufacturing.	
1792	*Letters to Married Women,* by Dr. Hugh Smith, becomes widely read book on nursing and child rearing.	
1794	Fashion of powdering men's hair goes out of style after over a century. Hair still worn long and tied in back.	
1797	Society for the Relief of Poor Widows with Small Children formed in New York.	
1801		Columbian Insurance Company formed in New York—beginning of trend.
1807		Congress passes law banning further African slave trade.
1811	Painting on velvet becomes popular among ladies.	
1816	About 66,000 women and girls and 34,000 men and boys, in cotton industry	
1818		Hannah Mather Crocker publishes *Observations on the Real Rights of Women.*
1820	Women constitute 90% of cotton industry.	
1821	Emma Willard opens Troy (N.Y.) Female Seminary (first women's high school).	

Date	Employment, Technology, Inventions, Health, Home, Morals, Fashion, Education	Achievements and Events, Woman Movement, Women's Liberation Movement, and Miscellaneous
1823–1827	Catharine Beecher runs girls' seminary, Hartford, Conn.	
1824	First recorded strike of women workers: Pawtucket, R.I. weavers	
1826		Nashoba, utopian community, formed near Memphis, Tenn., by Frances Wright.
1827	*Ladies' Magazine* founded by Mrs. Sarah Josepha Hale, first magazine specifically for women.	Mrs. Frances Trollope, writer and social commentator, arrives in U.S. from England.
ca. 1830	First cooking stoves marketed on regular basis in U.S.	Sojourner Truth is freed.
1831	Nat Turner Rebellion occurs.	
1832		Lydia Maria Child publishes *History of Women*.
1833	Oberlin becomes first co-ed college.	Lucretia Mott speaks at first convention of American Anti-Slavery Society in Philadelphia.
1833–1834	Prudence Crandall runs school for Negro girls in Connecticut.	
1836	Alonzo Phillips invents "striking match."	Temperance Union founded. Narcissa Prentiss Whitman and Eliza Hart Spaulding become first women to cross North America—in missionary expedition.
1837	*Exercise for Ladies*, by Donald Walker, cautions against horseback riding. *Manual for Politeness for Both Sexes*—becomes popular book. Mount Holyoke Seminary founded.	

Date	Employment, Technology, Inventions, Health, Home, Morals, Fashion, Education	Achievements and Events, Woman Movement, Women's Liberation Movement, and Miscellaneous
1837–1838		Grimké sisters become active in abolition and emerging woman movement.
1838	Georgia Female College begun as experiment in women's higher education. Mary Gove Nichols begins her anatomy lectures before female audiences.	Underground Railroad becomes well established. Angelina Grimké marries Theodore Weld.
1839		Josephine Amelia Perkins becomes first convicted lady horse thief.
1840		American Anti-Slavery Society sends delegates to London World Anti-Slavery Convention—women barred.
1843–1853		Dorothea Dix travels the country in drive to reform mental institutions.
1844		Margaret Fuller publishes *Woman in the Nineteenth Century*.
1845–1846	Sarah Bagley leads women workers at the Lowell, Mass. cotton mill.	
1846	Sewing machine invented by Elias Howe.	
1847	Beginning of standardized kitchen units. Catharine Beecher forms National Board of Popular Education.	Maria Mitchell discovers a comet, which is named after her.

Date	Employment, Technology, Inventions, Health, Home, Morals, Fashion, Education	Achievements and Events, Woman Movement, Women's Liberation Movement, and Miscellaneous
1848		Seneca Falls Woman's Rights Convention is held. New York legislature passes married women's property rights law. Maria Mitchell becomes first woman elected to American Academy of Arts and Sciences.
1849	Modern safety pin invented by Walter Hunt. Elizabeth Blackwell, M.D., admitted to practice in St. Bartholomew's Hospital, London. Boston Female Medical School founded; merges in 1874 with Boston University School of Medicine.	First issue of *Lily*, feminist journal, appears, edited by Amelia Bloomer.
1850	The iron range replaces the great hearth in settled areas. Amelia Bloomer begins to wear "bloomers," soon to become popular among active women, for short while. Women's Medical College of Pennsylvania founded.	Maria Mitchell becomes first woman elected to the Association for the Advancement of Science.
1851		Sojourner Truth delivers speech: ". . . Ain't I a Woman?"
1852	Most public-school teachers are women. Antioch College admits women. Antoinette Brown becomes first woman minister to be ordained.	Harriet Beecher Stowe publishes *Uncle Tom's Cabin*.

Date	Employment, Technology, Inventions, Health, Home, Morals, Fashion, Education	Achievements and Events, Woman Movement, Women's Liberation Movement, and Miscellaneous
1852	American Women's Educational Association formed by Catharine Beecher.	
1853	Women introduced as waitresses.	*Una*, feminist journal, appears.
1853–1876		*Woman's Record or Sketches of Distinguished Women* written by Mrs. Sarah Josepha Hale.
1855	Horseback riding is fashionable for ladies.	*The Woman Advocate*, feminist journal, founded by Mrs. Anna McDowell.
1857	Sewing machine perfected.	
1858	John L. Mason develops 3-part mason jar. H. C. Wright's *The Unwelcomed Child, or the Crime of an Undesigned and Undesired Maternity* becomes popular book on family planning. University of Iowa becomes first state university to admit women.	
1859	Home electrical lighting demonstration is given in Salem, Mass.	
1860	4 million slaves in the U.S. Olympia Brown admitted to St. Lawrence University, first woman studying theology on equal basis with men.	5,888,000 mulattoes estimated to be in the U.S. Tenth National Woman's Rights Convention has controversial debate on divorce. First English-language kindergarten established, in Boston.

Date	Employment, Technology, Inventions, Health, Home, Morals, Fashion, Education	Achievements and Events, Woman Movement, Women's Liberation Movement, and Miscellaneous
1861	Dorothea Dix becomes superintendent of women nurses, Union Army.	
1861– 1865		Mary Boykin Chesnut keeps wartime diary—*A Diary from Dixie*, published 1905.
1862	Jenny Douglas gets civil service job in Treasury Department; federal civil service opens to women.	Homestead Act encourages settling of the West. Congress enacts antipolygamy measure.
1863	Ebenezer Butterick invents first paper dress pattern sold in U.S.; 6 million sold by 1871. University of Wisconsin opens normal-school training course for women.	
1864	George M. Pullman introduces the *Pioneer*, a railroad sleeping car.	
1865	Beards become distinguished fashion for men after Civil War. Vassar College opens. Maria Mitchell becomes first woman professor of astronomy, at Vassar.	Thirteenth Amendment abolishes slavery.
1866	National Teachers' Association admits women on equal basis with men.	First U.S. YWCA opened, in Boston. American Society for the Prevention of Cruelty to Animals formed.

Date	Employment, Technology, Inventions, Health, Home, Morals, Fashion, Education	Achievements and Events, Woman Movement, Women's Liberation Movement, and Miscellaneous
1867	First practical typewriter constructed by Christopher L. Sholes. National Cigar Makers Union admits women.	Public schools made free to all children, not just to poor.
1868	*American Journal of Obstetrics* founded.	First measure proposing woman suffrage amendment introduced in Congress. Susan B. Anthony and Elizabeth Cady Stanton found *The Revolution*.
1868–1878	Female workers organize in Women's Typographical Union, Local No. 1.	
1869	Suction vacuum cleaner patented by I. W. McGaffey. Daughters of Saint Crispin (women's union) formed. Augusta Lewis organizes women typographers in New York. National Typographers Union admits women. Iowa allows women to practice law.	Arabella Mansfield becomes first woman lawyer (Iowa) since Margaret Brent. Catharine Beecher published *The American Woman's Home*. Sorosis, first women's club, founded by Jennie C. Croly in New York. New England Woman's Club founded in Boston. Territory of Wyoming grants woman suffrage. National Woman Suffrage Association founded. American Woman Suffrage Association founded.
1870	Myra Bradwell refused admission to Illinois Bar by state supreme court.	Territory of Utah enacts woman suffrage.

Date	Employment, Technology, Inventions, Health, Home, Morals, Fashion, Education	Achievements and Events, Woman Movement, Women's Liberation Movement, and Miscellaneous
1870		*Woman's Journal* begins publication as organ of American Woman Suffrage Association.
1872	Charlotte E. Ray graduates from Howard University Law School, first Negro woman lawyer.	Victoria Woodhull becomes first U.S. woman presidential candidate.
1873	Remington Arms Company perfects typewriter model. American Medical Association forms section on Obstetrics and Diseases of Women and Children. Comstock Law (federal anti-obscenity law) passed.	*Home Companion* (later *Woman's Home Companion*) begins publication; continues until 1957. First public kindergarten established. Susan B. Anthony put on trial for illegal voting.
1874	Sage College founded— women's branch of Cornell University.	Woman's Christian Temperance Union formed. Supreme Court upholds lower courts in deciding against the suit for woman suffrage brought by Mr. and Mrs. Minor. Henry Ward Beecher is sued for adultery; scandal rocks woman movement.
1876	Alexander Graham Bell invents telephone.	Five members of National Woman Suffrage Association, led by Susan B. Anthony, disrupt centennial celebrations in Philadelphia from which women had been barred from active participation.

Date	Employment, Technology, Inventions, Health, Home, Morals, Fashion, Education	Achievements and Events, Woman Movement, Women's Liberation Movement, and Miscellaneous
1877		Anti-Chinese riots in California, incited by Workingmen's Party.
1878	Practical application of electric lighting begun in Philadelphia.	Senator A. A. Sargent (California) introduces "Anthony Amendment" (for woman suffrage).
1879–1898		Frances Willard serves as president of Woman's Christian Temperance Union.
1881	Women admitted on equal basis with men to Knights of Labor. Clara Barton founds American Association of the Red Cross. American Association of University Women formed in Boston.	Jesse James and Billy the Kid shot. National organization of YWCAs founded. *History of Woman Suffrage*, vols. 1 and 2, published, ed. Elizabeth Cady Stanton, Susan B. Anthony, and M. J. Gage.
1882	Electric iron introduced.	Chinese Exclusion Act passed.
1884		Equal Rights Party founded, runs presidential candidate: Mrs. Belva A. Hockwood.
1885	Bryn Mawr College for Women opened.	
1885–1914		Number of immigrants to U.S. rises.
1886	U.S. has 266 colleges for women and over 250 other institutions of higher education that accept women.	Haymarket riot occurs in Chicago. *History of Woman Suffrage*, vol. 3 published, ed. Elizabeth Cady Stanton, Susan B. Anthony, and M. J. Gage.

Date	Employment, Technology, Inventions, Health, Home, Morals, Fashion, Education	Achievements and Events, Woman Movement, Women's Liberation Movement, and Miscellaneous
1889	Barnard College founded.	Hull House opens. Ida Wells, born of slave parents, edits *Memphis Free Speech*, paper that fights for Negro rights.
1890	Sewing machine and egg-beater constitute almost the only common mechanical aids to housework. 5% of married women are employed outside the home. About 603,000 children, 14 years or younger, are in the labor force. 23,000 children are employed as factory workers in the South. Almost one-half of women in U.S. live on farms.	General Federation of Women's Clubs formed. Wyoming becomes first state allowing woman suffrage, having granted it prior to statehood. National American Woman Suffrage Association formed. National Society of the Daughters of the American Revolution formed.
ca.1890		Colored Women's League founded, Washington, D.C.
1893	Ford builds first automobile. Mount Holyoke becomes a college.	Anti-Saloon League formed. World's Columbian Exposition (Chicago) has Woman's Building and active World Congress of Women.
1894	Theory of female costal vs. male abdominal breathing is disproved, revealing the damaging effects of tight corseting.	
1895	"Gibson Girl" arrives.	Convention of Negro women's clubs held in Boston. National Federation of Afro-American Women founded.

Date	Employment, Technology, Inventions, Health, Home, Morals, Fashion, Education	Achievements and Events, Woman Movement, Women's Liberation Movement, and Miscellaneous
1895		*The Woman's Bible*, pt. 1, published, ed. Elizabeth Cady Stanton.
ca.1895		New Era Club forms—Boston Negro women's organization. *The Woman's Era*, feminist journal of Negro women, appears.
1896	Electric stove invented.	7/8 of America's wealth controlled by 1/8 of the population. National Association of Colored Women formed.
1897	National Congress of Parents and Teachers founded.	Charlotte Perkins Gilman publishes *Women and Economics*.
1898		*The Woman's Bible*, pt. 2, published, ed. Elizabeth Cady Stanton.
1899		National Consumers' League formed. May Wood Simons publishes *Woman and the Social Question*.
1900	Local No. 131 of the United Garment Workers, San Francisco, formed. Later taken over by militant women. Proportion of women in cotton industry has fallen to 42% (cf. 1820 figure).	Average life expectancy is 50 years. Convention of General Federation of Women's Clubs rejects credentials of an active Negro club woman and feminist, Mrs. Josephine St. Pierre Ruffin.

179

Date	Employment, Technology, Inventions, Health, Home, Morals, Fashion, Education	Achievements and Events, Woman Movement, Women's Liberation Movement, and Miscellaneous
1900	U.S. has 432 schools of nursing (in 1873 there had been only 1).	Carry Nation begins anti-liquor crusade in Kansas. Susan B. Anthony retires.
1901	U.S. has 128 women's colleges.	Socialist Party of U.S. founded.
1902	Women constitute 25% of undergraduates, 26% of graduate students, 3% of professional students.	*History of Woman Suffrage*, vol. 4, published, ed. S. B. Anthony and I. H. Harper.
1903	Women's Trade Union League formed.	
1904	First female ushers employed, in New York City. National Child Labor Committee established. First union of stenographers and typists formed by Elise Diehl.	International Woman Suffrage Alliance formed.
1905		Pop song, "Everybody Works but Father," refers to increased employment of women.
1906–1917		Emma Goldman edits journal *Mother Earth*.
1907	U.S. Congress authorizes investigation of child and female labor.	First Mother's Day proclaimed.
1908	Smoking declared illegal for women in public places, New York City. "Sheath" becomes stylish (narrow skirt, worn without petticoats).	Isadora Duncan makes second grand American tour.
1910		Camp Fire Girls founded.

Date	Employment, Technology, Inventions, Health, Home, Morals, Fashion, Education	Achievements and Events, Woman Movement, Women's Liberation Movement, and Miscellaneous
1910–1911		Successful suffrage referenda held in Washington and California.
1910–1920	U.S. reports 103% increase of white women in clerical and sales work; 122% increase of black women in clerical and sales work; 4% increase of white women in industry. "Day of the Girl" and "Sex O'Clock in America" proclaimed.	
1911	Triangle Waist Company fire, New York City, kills 148, mostly girls and women.	
1912	Bread and Roses strike of female textile workers led by Elizabeth Gurley Flynn.	U.S. Children's Bureau established. Henrietta Leavitt (1868–1921) announces her "period-luminosity" law. Girl Scouts founded in U.S.
1913		Woman suffrage granted in Illinois. Harriet Tubman of the Underground Railroad dies a pauper.
1914	Profits surge in industries producing household appliances.	Congressional Union for Woman Suffrage formed by women who split off from the National American Woman Suffrage Association. Margaret Sanger edits journal *Woman Rebel*.
1915	Typewriter becomes standard office equipment.	*Family Limitation*, by Margaret Sanger, appears; author is jailed.

Date	Employment, Technology, Inventions, Health, Home, Morals, Fashion, Education	Achievements and Events, Woman Movement, Women's Liberation Movement, and Miscellaneous
1915		Carrie Chapman Catt heads suffrage movement in decisive period.
1916		Margaret Sanger, Fania Mindell, Ethel Burne open first birth control clinic,in Brooklyn.
		National Woman's Party formed in those states with woman suffrage.
1917		New York State adopts woman suffrage as constitutional amendment.
		Woman's Party pickets White House with slogan "Democracy Should Begin at Home,"; some are arrested.
		Rep. Jeannette Rankin, Republican from Montana, becomes first woman member in the House; casts sole vote against U.S. war involvement.
1918	Woman in Industry Service established, later to become U.S. Women's Bureau.	President Wilson tells Senate woman suffrage is vital to war effort.
	1916 Child Labor Act declared unconstitutional.	U.S. House adopts Susan B. Anthony (woman suffrage) resolution; it fails in Senate.
1919	Civil service opened to women on same basis as men.	Margaret B. Owens types a record 170 words per minute.
1919–1929	Automobile, chemical, electrical industries expand.	

Date	Employment, Technology, Inventions, Health, Home, Morals, Fashion, Education	Achievements and Events, Woman Movement, Women's Liberation Movement, and Miscellaneous
1920	Consumption of canned foods, store-bought baked goods, and delicatessen food rises. Age of the "Flapper" dawns.	U.S. Women's Bureau established. Nineteenth Amendment to the U.S. Constitution (Woman Suffrage Amendment), passed.
1920–1933		Prohibition becomes law of the land.
1921	First Miss America Contest held.	First immigration quota law passed. American Birth Control League founded by Margaret Sanger. Dr. Marie Stopes arrested for her book *Married Love*, which discusses contraception.
1922	Knee-length skirts for women become fashionable. 3 million homes have radios.	Mrs. W. H. Felton becomes first woman in U.S. Senate—term lasts 1 day. *History of Woman Suffrage*, vols. 5 and 6, published, ed. I. H. Harper.
1925	Charleston dance becomes popular.	
1926	Sarah Lawrence College for Women founded.	Aimee Semple MacPherson becomes nationally known revivalist. Gertrude Ederle of New York becomes first woman to swim English Channel (at age 19).
1927		First full-length talking movie is made.
1928		Amelia Earhart becomes first woman to fly Atlantic.

Date	Employment, Technology, Inventions, Health, Home, Morals, Fashion, Education	Achievements and Events, Woman Movement, Women's Liberation Movement, and Miscellaneous
1930	47% of undergraduates are women; 28% of Ph.D.'s are women.	
1931	Depression leaves 26.2% of men unemployed, 18.9% of women unemployed.	
1932	*The Nation* devotes January 27 issue to birth control.	
1933– 1936	Strikes, labor agitation increase.	"Dust Bowl" states suffer from severe droughts.
1935	Appliance industry turns toward the streamlined-kitchen concept. Social Security Act creates new group: welfare families.	*Journal of Contraception* begun by Margaret Sanger. General Federation of Women's Clubs reverses earlier stand and endorses federal law allowing mailing of birth control information.
1936	160,000 trailers are on the road in the "age of trailers."	King Edward VIII of England abdicates out of love for Mrs. Wallis Warfield Simpson, an American.
1938	Patents issued for nylon; commercial products made from nylon soon follow.	Pearl S. Buck wins Nobel Prize for Literature.
1940s	Fertility of American women emphasized. World War II: 130,000 children placed in over 3,000 day-care centers.	
1940	Major household appliances in plumbing, lighting, fuel become common in cities.	Life expectancy has risen to 64, up from around 50 in 1900.

Date	Employment, Technology, Inventions, Health, Home, Morals, Fashion, Education	Achievements and Events, Woman Movement, Women's Liberation Movement, and Miscellaneous
1940	Women's entry into work force accelerates. 15% of married women work. Nylon stockings first go on sale.	
1942	"Momism" popular; social critics blame American women for nation's maladies. Lanham Act passed, allotting federal funds for wartime day care.	
1942–1943		Women's Army Auxiliary Corps, Women Accepted for Volunteer Emergency Service, Women's Auxiliary Ferrying Squadron, Women's Reserve of the Coast Guard, Women's Reserve of the U.S. Marines formed.
1943	Jitterbug becomes popular.	
1945–1947	Number of women in labor force drops from 20.3 million to 15.9 million.	
1946	Trend of ranch-style and split-level homes begins.	Emily Greene Balch wins Nobel Peace Prize (founder of Women's International League for Peace and Freedom).
1947	TV goes on the market. *Modern Woman, the Lost Sex*, by Ferdinand Lundberg and Marynia F. Farnham, published: popular antifeminist book.	
1948	Alfred Kinsey's *Sexual Behavior in the Human Male* published.	

Date	Employment, Technology, Inventions, Health, Home, Morals, Fashion, Education	Achievements and Events, Woman Movement, Women's Liberation Movement, and Miscellaneous
1940–1950	100% increase of white women in industry reported; also 76% increase of white women in farm labor, 138% increase of black women in white-collar sector (348% increase of black women in clerical and sales work), 334% increase of black women as skilled workers and foremen	
1951	Employment of women reaches new peak: 19,308,000.	
1953	Alfred Kinsey's *Sexual Behavior of Human Female* published.	*The Second Sex*, by Simone de Beauvoir, appears in American edition.
1954	3 out of 5 American homes have TV sets.	
1955	Tranquilizers begin to be used extensively.	Marian Anderson makes first Metropolitan Opera appearance. Rosa Parks begins drive for desegregation of buses in Montgomery, Ala.
1956	Autherine Lucy enrolls at University of Alabama, first Negro.	Maria Callas makes debut at the Met. Grace Kelly marries Prince Rainier III of Monaco.
1957	The "sack" becomes a women's fashion.	
1958		National Defense Education Act passed.
1958–1968	Union membership among women workers declines from 13.8% to 12.5%.	

Date	Employment, Technology, Inventions, Health, Home, Morals, Fashion, Education	Achievements and Events, Woman Movement, Women's Liberation Movement, and Miscellaneous
1959		Lorraine H. Hansberry first Negro to receive New York Drama Critics Circle Award, for *A Raisin in the Sun*.
1960–1970	Women hold 65.3% of 11.9 million jobs added to work force. Proportion of jobs held by women increases from 33% to 38%. Women fill nearly 50% of new jobs in editing and reporting, for a total of 40% of the field. Clerical jobs rise by 3.8 million. Number of maids drops to 546,000. Women constitute only 12% of all insurance agents. Women hold 58% of new real estate jobs, for a total of 32%. Women account for only 3.5% of the job gain in engineering. Women fill 121% of new bartending jobs, to become 21% of the total. 75% of bus driver jobs added are filled by women. Contraceptive pill achieves mass acceptance.	
1961	Aid to Families with Dependent Children extends welfare.	Women Strike for Peace organized. President's Commission on the Status of Women established.

Date	Employment, Technology, Inventions, Health, Home, Morals, Fashion, Education	Achievements and Events, Woman Movement, Women's Liberation Movement, and Miscellaneous
1961 cont.		Elizabeth Gurley Flynn becomes first woman national chairman of U.S. Communist Party.
1961– 1962	Thalidomide is exposed as dangerous drug.	
1962		Marilyn Monroe dies. *American Women: the Changing Image,* ed. Beverly Cassara, published. U.S. emerges from antifeminism of 1940s and 1950s.
1963		Equal Pay Act passed, covering women as well as men. *Feminine Mystique,* by Betty Friedan, published. Interdepartmental Committee on the Status of Women, and Citizens' Advisory Council on the Status of Women formed. Hope Cooke marries Crown Prince Palden Thondup Namgyal of Sikkim.
1964		Civil Rights Act bans sex discrimination in employment. Ruby Doris Robinson raises women's issue within SNCC. Fannie Lou Hamer and Ruby Doris Robinson lead Freedom Democratic Party at Democratic National Convention.

Date	Employment, Technology, Inventions, Health, Home, Morals, Fashion, Education	Achievements and Events, Woman Movement, Women's Liberation Movement, and Miscellaneous
1965	One-fifth of children under 14 need day care, under 5% are in licensed centers.	
1965–1966		Women raising the women's issue meet abuse at SDS convention.
1966	Miniskirt becomes fashionable	*Human Sexual Response,* by Masters and Johnson, published.
		National Organization of Women founded.
		Eight student nurses murdered in Chicago.
		Drugs become national topic.
1966–1968		Women's liberation movement emerges.
1967		National Welfare Rights Organization founded.
		First "Be-In" held, at Golden Gate Park, San Francisco.
		Jeannette Rankin Brigade March on Washington to Protest the Vietnam War takes place.
1968	37% of married women work in labor force.	Congresswoman Shirley Chisolm elected.
	Work Incentive Program (WIN) added to welfare system.	Women's Equity Action League founded.
	TWA stewardesses begin drive for organization in their occupation.	Women's liberation's first national conference held, in Chicago.
	2.9% unemployment reported among men, officially, and 4.8% unemployment among women; 50% of unemployed workers are women.	Miss America Contest picketed.

Date	Employment, Technology, Inventions, Health, Home, Morals, Fashion, Education	Achievements and Events, Woman Movement, Women's Liberation Movement, and Miscellaneous
1968	Federally Employed Women formed.	*Voice of the Women's Liberation Movement* (Chicago) becomes first movement journal. Women's International Terrorist Conspiracy from Hell (WITCH) formed. The Feminists (New York) organized. *Notes from the First Year* published by New York Radical Women.
1969	Average earnings in professional and technical fields show men with $12,262 and women with $5,927 (or 48% of male earnings). Nixon proposes Family Assistance Plan, welfare reform. Two-thirds of American women are reported not in labor force.	Presidential Task Force on Women's Rights and Responsibilities presents radical report: *A Matter of Simple Justice.* U.S. Women's Bureau advocates Equal Rights Amendment. Equal Employment Opportunity Commission declares protective legislation illegal when applied exclusively to women. Redstockings founded. Gay Liberation Front formed. Church women organize. Bread and Roses (Boston) formed. Women's caucuses formed in American Sociological Association, American Political Science Association, American Psychological Association, Modern Language Association.

Date	Employment, Technology, Inventions, Health, Home, Morals, Fashion, Education	Achievements and Events, Woman Movement, Women's Liberation Movement, and Miscellaneous
1969		New York Radical Feminists founded.
1970	Percentage of single women at marriageable age rises more than 10%.	Women's Bureau puts out *1969 Handbook on Women Workers.*
	National fertility study shows almost zero population growth.	August 26, first national women's strike declared: 50th anniversary of passage of Suffrage Amendment.
	138 male midwives reported in practice.	
	756 women reported working as telephone linemen.	Uprisings take place among women on staffs of *Newsweek; Ladies' Home Journal;* Time, Inc.
	Women still constitute only 10% of lawyers and judges.	
	First state AFL–CIO Women's Conference held, in Wisconsin Rapids, Wis.	Governmental agencies and American Association of University Professors scrutinize status of women in universities.
	Medical problems of contraceptive pill gain wide public attention.	50th anniversary of U.S. Women's Bureau celebrated.
	Feminine hygiene spray introduced.	*Sexual Politics,* by Kate Millett, published.
	Abortion law repealed in Hawaii.	Angela Davis arrested.
1971	38% of undergraduates are women; 13% of Ph.D.'s are women.	Supreme Court makes first ruling on sex discrimination in view of 1964 Civil Rights Act. Women with preschool children shall receive equal treatment in the labor force.
	About 55 colleges and universities offer courses in women's studies.	
		National Women's Political Caucus organized.
		Rising consciousness of the problem of rape and other crimes against women.

Date	Employment, Technology, Inventions, Health, Home, Morals, Fashion, Education	Achievements and Events, Woman Movement, Women's Liberation Movement, and Miscellaneous
1972	750,000 children receive day care service in licensed centers, which represents steady increase from 650,000 in 1969 and 500,000 in 1967. Washington, D.C., stewardesses organize Stewardesses for Women's Rights. Backlash against hiring of women in higher education occurs. Nixon vetoes day care bill. Birthrate dips below low depression level.	*Ms.* magazine founded. Women's liberation is a minor issue at the Democratic National Convention.
1973	Supreme Court legalizes abortion, except for certain cases.	

SELECTED
BIBLIOGRAPHY

Articles, Reports, and Pamphlets

Bem, S. L., and D. J. Bem. "Case Study of a Nonconscious Ideology: Training the Woman to Know Her Place." In D. J. Bem, *Beliefs, Attitudes, and Human Affairs.* Belmont, Calif.: Brooks/Cole, 1970.

Blackburn, Robin, and Lucien Rey. "Two Comments: Responses to Branka Magas' Article on 'Sex Politics: Class Politics.'" *New Left Review,* no. 66 (March–April 1971), pp. 92–96.

Boyer, Susan. "The Day Care Jungle." *Saturday Review,* February 20, 1971, pp. 50–51.

Brown, Emily C. *Industrial Home Work.* U.S. Women's Bureau, Department of Labor, Bulletin no. 79, 1930.

Buhle, Mari Jo, Ann G. Gordon, and Nancy Schrom. "Women in American Society: An Historical Contribution." *Radical America* 5, no. 4 (July–August 1971): 3–66.

Butler, Elizabeth Beardsley. "The Industrial Environment of Pittsburgh's Working Women." *Charities* 21 (1908–1909): 117–142.

——. "Pittsburgh Women in the Metal Trades." *Charities* 21 (1908–1909): 34–47.

Caldwell, Bettye M. 'A Timid Giant Grows Bolder." *Saturday Review,* February 20, 1971, pp. 47–66.

Child Care Services Provided by Hospitals. U.S. Women's Bureau, Department of Labor, Bulletin no. 295, 1970.

Children of Wage-earning Mothers. Children's Bureau, U.S. Department of Health, Education, and Welfare, 1922.

Day Care Services: Industry's Involvement. U.S. Women's Bureau, Department of Labor, Bulletin no. 296, 1971.

Dempsey, Mary V. *The Occupational Progress of Women, 1910 to 1930.* U.S. Women's Bureau, Department of Labor, Bulletin no. 104, 1933.

Dewey, Lucretia M. "Women in Labor Unions." *Monthly Labor Review* 94, no. 2 (February 1971): 42–48.

The Effects of Labor Legislation on the Employment Opportunities of Women. U.S. Women's Bureau, Department of Labor, Bulletin no. 65, 1928.

Employed Mothers and Child Care. U.S. Women's Bureau, Department of Labor, Bulletin no. 246, 1953.

Employment of Women in an Emergency Period. U.S. Women's Bureau, Department of Labor, Bulletin, no. 241, 1952.

Everett, Laura B. "High School Nurseries." *Survey* 57 (March 15, 1927): 804.

Fact Finding with the Women's Bureau. U.S. Women's Bureau, Department of Labor, Bulletin no. 84, 1931.

Facts about Working Women. U.S. Women's Bureau, Department of Labor, Bulletin no. 46, 1925.

Featherstone, Joseph. "The Day Care Problem: Kentucky Fried Children." *New Republic,* September 12, 1970, pp. 12–16.

Federal Funds for Day Care Projects. U.S. Women's Bureau, Department of Labor, 1969.

Goldfield, Evelyn, Sue Munaker, and Naomi Weisstein. "A Woman is a Sometime Thing." In *The New Left,* edited by Priscilla Long, pp. 236–271. Boston Porter Sargent, 1969.

Gray, Betty MacMorran. "Economics of Sex Bias: The Disuse of Women." *Nation,* June 14, 1971, pp. 742–744.

Hacker, Helen. "Women as a Minority Group." *Social Forces* 30 (October 1951): 60–69.

Hewes, Amy. *Women Workers in the Third Year of the Depression—Study by Students of the Bryn Mawr Summer School.* U.S. Women's Bureau, Department of Labor, Bulletin, no. 103, 1933.

Home Environment and Employment Opportunities of Women in Coal-Mine Workers' Families. U.S. Women's Bureau, Department of Labor, 1925.

Hooks, Janet M. *Women's Occupations Through Seven Decades.* U.S. Women's Bureau, Department of Labor, Bulletin no. 218, 1947.

The Immigrant Woman and Her Job. U.S. Women's Bureau, Department of Labor, Bulletin no. 74, 1930.

Lerner, Gerda. "The Lady and the Mill Girl: Changes in the Status of Women in the Age of Jackson." *Mid-Continent American Studies Journal* (Spring 1970): 45-66.

Low, Seth, and Pearl G. Spindler. *Child Care Arrangements of Working Mothers in the United States.* Children's Bureau, Social and Rehabilitation Service, U.S. Department of Health, Education, and Welfare, Bulletin no. 461, 1968.

Matthews, Lillian R. "Women in Trade Unions in San Francisco." *University of California in Economics,* 3, no. 1 (1913): 1-100.

Mitchell, Juliet. "The Longest Revolution." *New Left Review,* no. 40 (November-December 1966), pp. 11-37.

Negro Women in Industry. U.S. Women's Bureau, Department of Labor, 1922.

Pidgeon, Mary Elizabeth. *Women in the Economy of the United States of America.* U.S. Women's Bureau, Department of Labor, Bulletin no. 155, 1937.

Prescott, Elizabeth, and Elizabeth Jones. "Day Care for Children: Assets and Liabilities." *Children,* March-April 1971, pp. 54-58.

Proceedings of Conference on Day Care of Children of Working Mothers, Washington, D.C., July 31 and August 1, 1941. Children's Bureau, Social and Rehabilitation Service, U.S. Department of Health, Education, and Welfare, Bulletin no. 281, 1942.

Rothman, Sheila M. "Other People's Children: The Day Care Experience in America." *Public Interest,* no. 30 (Winter 1973), pp. 11-27.

Valmeras, L. "The Work Community." *Radical America* 5, no. 4 (July-August 1971): 77-92.

Wells, Robert V. "Demographic Change and the Life Cycle of American Families." *Journal of Interdisciplinary History* 2 (Autumn 1971): 273-282.

Welter, Barbara. "The Cult of True Womanhood." *American Quarterly* 18 (1966): 151-174.

Books

Abbott, Edith. *Women in Industry.* New York: D. Appleton, 1910.

Adams, Elizabeth Kemper. *Women Professional Workers.* New York: Macmillan, 1921.

Adams, Elsie, and Mary Louise Briscoe. *Up Against the Wall, Mother....* Beverly Hills, Calif.: Glencoe Press, 1971.

Allen, Ruth Alice. *The Labor of Women in the Production of Cotton.* Chicago: Private Edition, distributed by the University of Chicago Libraries, 1933.

Altbach, Edith Hoshino, ed. *From Feminism to Liberation.* Cambridge, Mass.: Schenkman, 1971.

Amundsen, Kirsten. *The Silenced Majority: Women and American Democracy.* Englewood Cliffs, N.J.: Prentice-Hall, 1971.

Anderson, Mary. *Woman at Work.* Minneapolis: University of Minnesota Press, 1951.

Andrews, John B., and W. D. P. Bliss. *History of Women in Trade Unions.* Washington, D.C.: Government Printing Office, 1911.

Astin, Helen S. *The Woman Doctorate in America.* New York: Russell Sage Foundation, 1969.

Baker, Elizabeth Faulkner. *Technology and Woman's Work.* New York: Columbia University Press, 1964.

Beard, Mary R. *America Through Women's Eyes.* New York: Macmillan, 1933.

_____ . *Woman as a Force in History.* New York: Macmillan, 1946.

Beauvoir, Simone de. *The Second Sex.* New York: Bantam Books, 1961.

Beecher, Catharine E. *Woman's Profession as Mother and Educator, with Views in Opposition to Woman Suffrage.* Philadelphia: George Maclean, 1872.

Bernard, Jessie. *Academic Women.* University Park, Pa.: Pennsylvania State University Press, 1964.

Bird, Caroline. *Born Female. The High Cost of Keeping Women Down.* New York: David McKay, 1968.

Buehr, Walter. *Home Sweet Home in the Nineteenth Century.* New York: Thomas Y. Crowell, 1965.

Burks, John, and Jerry Hopkins. *Groupies and Other Girls.* Edited by Jann Wenner. New York: Bantam Books, 1970.

Cade, Toni, ed. *The Black Woman.* New York: Signet Books, New American Library, 1970.

Cassara, Beverly Benner, ed. *American Women: The Changing Image.* Boston: Beacon Press, 1962.

196

Chesnut, Mary Boykin. *A Diary from Dixie.* Edited by B. A. Williams. 1905. Reprint. Boston: Houghton Mifflin, 1949.

Coser, Rose L., ed. *The Family: Its Structure and Functions.* New York: St. Martin's Press, 1964.

Crocker, Hannah Mather. *Observations on the Real Rights of Women.* Boston, 1818.

Croly, Jennie C. *The History of the Woman's Club Movement in America.* New York: H. G. Allen, 1898.

Cross, Barbara M. *The Educated Woman in America. Selected Writings of Catharine Beecher, Margaret Fuller, and M. Carey Thomas.* New York: Teachers College Press, Columbia University, 1965.

Dahlström, Edmund, ed. *The Changing Roles of Men and Women.* Boston: Beacon Press, 1971.

Dexter, Elisabeth A. *Colonial Women of Affairs.* Boston: Houghton Mifflin, 1924.

Dingwall, Eric John. *The American Woman. An Historical Study.* New York: Rinehart, 1956.

Ditzion, Sidney. *Marriage Morals and Sex in America. A History of Ideas.* New York: Bookman Associates, 1953.

Drinnon, Richard. *Rebel in Paradise. A Biography of Emma Goldman.* Boston: Beacon Press, 1970.

Duniway, Abigail Scott. *Path Breaking: An autobiographical history of the equal suffrage movement in Pacific Coast states, with new introduction by Eleanor Flexner.* 1914. Reprint. New York: Schocken Books, 1971.

Earle, Alice M. *Colonial Dames and Good Wives.* New York: Frederick Ungar, 1962.

Epstein, Cynthia Fuchs. *Woman's Place. Options and Limits in Professional Careers.* Berkeley: University of California Press, 1970.

Evans, E. Belle, and Marlene Weinstein. *Day Care: How to Plan, Develop, and Operate a Day Care Center.* Boston: Beacon Press, 1971.

Evans, E. Belle, and George E. Saia. *Day Care for Infants. The Case for Infant Day Care and a Practical Guide.* Boston: Beacon Press, 1972.

Farber, Seymour M., and Roger H. L. Wilson, eds. *The Potential of Woman.* New York: McGraw Hill Paperbacks, 1963.

Firestone, Shulamith. *The Dialectic of Sex. The Case for Feminist Revolution.* New York: William Morrow, 1970.

Flexner, Eleanor. *Century of Struggle.* New York: Atheneum, 1970.

Friedan, Betty. *The Feminine Mystiqué.* New York: Dell, 1963.

Giedion, Siegfried. *Mechanization Takes Command. A Contribution to Anonymous History.* New York: W. N. Norton, 1969.

Gilbreth, Lillian M., Orpha Mae Thomas, and Eleanor Clymer. *Management in the Home.* New York: Dodd, Mead, 1959.

Gilman, Charlotte Perkins. *The Home, Its Work and Influence.* New York: McClure, Phillips, 1903.

_____. *The Man-Made World, or Our Androcentric Culture.* New York: Charlton, 1911.

_____. *Women and Economics. A Study of the Economic Relation as a Factor in Social Evolution.* Edited by Carl N. Degler. 1898. Reprint. New York: Harper & Row, 1966.

Ginzberg, Eli, et al. *Educated American Women: Life Styles and Self Portraits.* New York: Columbia University Press, 1966.

Good Housekeeping's Guide to Successful Homemaking. New York: Harper and Brothers, 1961.

Gornick, Vivian, and Barbara K. Moran. *Woman in Sexist Society. Studies in Power and Powerlessness.* New York: Basic Books, 1971.

Groves, Ernest R. *The American Woman.* New York: Emerson Books, 1944.

Hagood, Margaret Jarman. *Mothers of the South.* Chapel Hill: University of North Carolina Press, 1939.

Henry, Alice. *The Trade Union Woman.* New York: D. Appleton, 1915.

_____. *Women and the Labor Movement.* New York: George H. Doran, 1923.

Herschberger, Ruth. *Adam's Rib.* New York: Pellegrini and Cudahy, 1948.

Hiestand, Dale L. *Economic Growth and Employment Opportunities for Minorities.* New York: Columbia University Press, 1964.

Hole, Judith, and Ellen Levine. *Rebirth of Feminism.* New York: Quadrangle Books, 1971.

Hutchins, Grace. *Women Who Work.* New York: International Publishers, 1934.

Jensen, Oliver. *The Revolt of American Women. A Pictorial History of the Century of Change from Bloomers to Bikinis—from Feminism to Freud.* New York: Harcourt, Brace, 1952.

Josephson, Hannah. *Golden Threads.* New York: Duell, Sloan and Pearce, 1949.

Komarovsky, Mirra. *Blue-Collar Marriage.* New York: Vintage Books, 1967.

Komarovsky, Mirra. *Women in the Modern World. Their Education and Their Dilemmas.* Boston: Little, Brown, 1953.

Kraditor, Aileen S. *The Ideas of the Woman Suffrage Movement 1890–1920.* New York: Columbia University Press, 1965.

Kraditor, Aileen S., ed. *Up from the Pedestal. Selected Writings in the History of American Feminism.* Chicago: Quadrangle Books, 1968.

Lerner, Gerda. *The Grimké Sisters from South Carolina. Pioneers for Woman's Rights and Abolition.* New York: Schocken Books, 1971.

Leonard, Eugenie Andrews. *The Dear-Bought Heritage.* Philadelphia: University of Pennsylvania Press, 1965.

Lifton, Robert Jay, ed. *The Woman in America.* Boston: Beacon Press, 1967.

Lynd, Robert S., and Helen Merrell Lynd. *Middletown.* New York: Harcourt, Brace, 1929.

Millett, Kate. *Sexual Politics.* New York: Doubleday, 1970.

Mitchell, Juliet. *Woman's Estate.* New York: Pantheon Books, 1971.

Morgan, Edmund S. *The Puritan Family: Essays on Religious and Domestic Relations in Seventeenth-Century New England.* Boston: Trustees of the Public Library, 1944.

Morgan, Robin, ed. *Sisterhood Is Powerful.* New York: Vintage Books, 1970.

1969 Handbook on Women Workers. U.S. Women's Bureau, Department of Labor, 1969.

O'Gorman, Ned. *The Storefront. A Community of Children on 129th Street and Madison Avenue.* New York: Torchbooks, Harper & Row, 1970.

O'Neil, William L. *Everyone Was Brave: The Rise and Fall of Feminism in America.* New York: Quadrangle Books, 1968.

Oppenheimer, Valerie Kincade. *The Female Labor Force in the United States. Demographic and Economic Factors Governing Its Growth and Changing Composition.* Berkeley: Institute of International Studies, University of California, 1970.

Papashvily, Helen W. *All the Happy Endings.* New York: Harper & Row, 1956.

Rainwater, Lee, Richard P. Coleman, and Gerald Handel. *Workingman's Wife.* New York: Oceana Publications, 1959.

Roszak, Betty, and Theodore Roszak, eds. *Masculine/Feminine. Readings in Sexual Mythology and the Liberation of Women.* New York: Harper & Row, 1969.

Salper, Roberta, ed. *Female Liberation. History and Current Politics.* New York: Alfred A. Knopf, 1972.

Scott, Anne Firor. *The Southern Lady from Pedestal to Politics 1830–1930.* Chicago: University of Chicago Press, 1970.

Scott, Anne Firor, ed. *The American Woman: Who Was She?* Englewood Cliffs, N.J.: Prentice-Hall, 1971.

Showalter, Elaine. *Women's Liberation and Literature.* New York: Harcourt Brace Jovanovich, 1971.

Sinclair, Andrew. *The Better Half.* New York: Harper & Row, 1965.

Smuts, Robert W. *Women and Work in America.* New York: Columbia University Press, 1959.

Spruill, Julia C. *Woman's Life and Work in the Southern Colonies.* Chapel Hill: University of North Carolina Press, 1938.

Stambler, Sookie, ed. *Women's Liberation Blueprint for the Future.* New York: Ace Books, 1970.

Stanton, Elizabeth Cady. *Eighty Years and More.* 1898. Reprint. New York: Schocken Books, 1971.

Tanner, Leslie B., ed. *Voices from Women's Liberation.* New York: Signet Books, New American Library, 1970.

Theodore, Athena, ed. *The Professional Woman.* Cambridge, Mass.: Schenkman, 1971.

Thompson, Mary Lou, ed. *Voices of the New Feminism.* Boston: Beacon Press, 1970.

Vigman, Fred. *Beauty's Triumph.* Boston: Christopher, 1966.

Ware, Cellestine. *Woman Power: The Movement for Women's Liberation.* New York: Tower, 1970.

Watkins, Mel, and David Jay, eds. *To Be a Black Woman.* New York: William Morrow, 1970.

Wolfson, Theresa. *The Woman Worker and the Trade Unions.* New York: International Publishers, 1926.

Wright, Lawrence. *Home Fires Burning. The History of Domestic Heating and Cooking.* London: Routledge and Kegan Paul, 1964.

INDEX